Alastair Riddell's Space Waltz

33 1/3 Global

33 1/3 Global, a series related to but independent from **33 1/3**, takes the format of the original series of short, music-based books and brings the focus to music throughout the world. With initial volumes focusing on Japanese and Brazilian music, the series will also include volumes on the popular music of Australia/Oceania, Europe, Africa, the Middle East, and more.

33 1/3 Japan

Series Editor: Noriko Manabe

Spanning a range of artists and genres – from the 1970s rock of Happy End to technopop band Yellow Magic Orchestra, the Shibuya-kei of Cornelius, classic anime series *Cowboy Bebop*, J-Pop/EDM hybrid Perfume, and vocaloid star Hatsune Miku – **33 1/3 Japan** is a series devoted to in-depth examination of Japanese popular music of the twentieth and twenty-first centuries.

Published Titles:
Supercell's *Supercell* by Keisuke Yamada
AKB48 by Patrick W. Galbraith and Jason G. Karlin
Yoko Kanno's *Cowboy Bebop Soundtrack* by Rose Bridges
Perfume's *Game* by Patrick St. Michel
Cornelius's *Fantasma* by Martin Roberts
Joe Hisaishi's *My Neighbor Totoro: Soundtrack* by Kunio Hara
Shonen Knife's *Happy Hour* by Brooke McCorkle
Nenes' *Koza Dabasa* by Henry Johnson
Yuming's *The 14th Moon* by Lasse Lehtonen

Forthcoming Titles:
Yellow Magic Orchestra's *Yellow Magic Orchestra* by Toshiyuki Ohwada
Kohaku utagassen: The Red and White Song Contest by Shelley Brunt

33 1/3 Brazil

Series Editor: Jason Stanyek

Covering the genres of samba, tropicália, rock, hip hop, forró, bossa nova, heavy metal and funk, among others, **33 1/3 Brazil** is a series devoted to in-depth examination of the most important Brazilian albums of the twentieth and twenty-first centuries.

Published Titles:
Caetano Veloso's *A Foreign Sound* by Barbara Browning
Tim Maia's *Tim Maia Racional Vols. 1 &2* by Allen Thayer
João Gilberto and Stan Getz's *Getz/Gilberto* by Brian McCann
Gilberto Gil's *Refazenda* by Marc A. Hertzman
Dona Ivone Lara's *Sorriso Negro* by Mila Burns
Milton Nascimento and Lô Borges's *The Corner Club* by Jonathon Grasse
Racionais MCs' *Sobrevivendo no Inferno* by Derek Pardue
Naná Vasconcelos's *Saudades* by Daniel B. Sharp
Chico Buarque's First *Chico Buarque* by Charles A. Perrone

Forthcoming titles:
Jorge Ben Jor's *África Brasil* by Frederick J. Moehn

33 1/3 Europe

Series Editor: Fabian Holt

Spanning a range of artists and genres, **33 1/3 Europe** offers engaging accounts of popular and culturally significant albums of Continental Europe and the North Atlantic from the twentieth and twenty-first centuries.

Published Titles:
Darkthrone's *A Blaze in the Northern Sky* by Ross Hagen
Ivo Papazov's *Balkanology* by Carol Silverman
Heiner Müller and Heiner Goebbels's *Wolokolamsker Chaussee* by Philip V. Bohlman
Modeselektor's *Happy Birthday!* by Sean Nye
Mercyful Fate's *Don't Break the Oath* by Henrik Marstal
Bea Playa's *I'll Be Your Plaything* by Anna Szemere and András Rónai
Various Artists' *DJs do Guetto* by Richard Elliott
Czesław Niemen's *Niemen Enigmatic* by Ewa Mazierska and Mariusz Gradowski

Massada's *Astaganaga* by Lutgard Mutsaers
Los Rodriguez's *Sin Documentos* by Fernán del Val and Héctor Fouce
Édith Piaf's *Récital 1961* by David Looseley
Nuovo Canzoniere Italiano's *Bella Ciao* by Jacopo Tomatis
Iannis Xenakis' *Persepolis* by Aram Yardumian

Forthcoming Titles:
Amália Rodrigues's *Amália at the Olympia* by Lila Ellen Gray
Ardit Gjebrea's *Projekt Jon* by Nicholas Tochka
Vopli Vidopliassova's *Tantsi* by Maria Sonevytsky

33 1/3 Oceania
Series Editors: Jon Stratton (senior editor) and Jon Dale (specializing
in books on albums from Aotearoa/New Zealand)
Spanning a range of artists and genres from Australian Indigenous
artists to Maori and Pasifika artists, from Aotearoa/New Zealand noise
music to Australian rock, and including music from Papua and other
Pacific islands, **33 1/3 Oceania** offers exciting accounts of albums
that illustrate the wide range of music made in the Oceania region.

Published Titles:
John Farnham's *Whispering Jack* by Graeme Turner
The Church's *Starfish* by Chris Gibson
Regurgitator's *Unit* by Lachlan Goold and Lauren Istvandity
Kylie Minogue's *Kylie* by Adrian Renzo and Liz Giuffre
Alastair Riddell's *Space Waltz* by Ian Chapman

Forthcoming Titles:
Ed Kuepper's *Honey Steel's Gold* by John Encarnacao
The Dead C's *Clyma est mort* by Darren Jorgensen
Chain's *Toward the Blues* by Peter Beilharz
Bic Runga's *Drive* by Henry Johnson
The Front Lawn's *Songs from the Front Lawn* by Matthew Bannister
Hilltop Hoods' *The Calling* by Dianne Rodger
Hunters & Collectors's *Human Frailty* by Jon Stratton
Screamfeeder's *Kitten Licks* by Ben Green and Ian Rogers
Luke Rowell's *Buy Now* by Michael Brown

Alastair Riddell's Space Waltz

Ian Chapman

Series Editors: Jon Stratton, UniSA Creative, University of South Australia, and Jon Dale, University of Melbourne, Australia

BLOOMSBURY ACADEMIC

NEW YORK · LONDON · OXFORD · NEW DELHI · SYDNEY

BLOOMSBURY ACADEMIC
Bloomsbury Publishing Inc
1385 Broadway, New York, NY 10018, USA
50 Bedford Square, London, WC1B 3DP, UK
29 Earlsfort Terrace, Dublin 2, Ireland

BLOOMSBURY, BLOOMSBURY ACADEMIC and the Diana logo are trademarks of Bloomsbury Publishing Plc

First published in the United States of America 2023

Copyright © Ian Chapman, 2023

For legal purposes the Acknowledgements on p. xi constitute an extension of this copyright page.

Lyrics used by permission of Alastair Riddell.

Cover design: Louise Dugdale
Cover credit © 333sound.com

Library of Congress Cataloging-in-Publication Data

Names: Chapman, Ian, 1960- author.
Title: Space Waltz / Ian Chapman.
Description: New York, NY : Bloomsbury Academic, 2023. | Series: 33 1/3 Oceania | Includes bibliographical references and index. | Summary: "Explores the career and one-album output of Space Waltz, a short-lived New Zealand glam rock band with a #1 hit song that was a vehicle for singer-songwriter Alastair Riddell"– Provided by publisher.
Identifiers: LCCN 2022043092 (print) | LCCN 2022043093 (ebook) | ISBN 9781501389504 (hardback) | ISBN 9781501389511 (paperback) | ISBN 9781501389528 (epub) | ISBN 9781501389535 (pdf) | ISBN 9781501389542 (ebook other)
Subjects: LCSH: Space Waltz (Musical group). Space Waltz by Alastair Riddell. | Rock music–New Zealand–1971-1980–History and criticism. | Glam rock (Music)–New Zealand– History and criticism.
Classification: LCC ML421.S658 C53 2023 (print) | LCC ML421.S658 (ebook) | DDC 782.42166092/2–dc23/eng/20220906
LC record available at https://lccn.loc.gov/2022043092
LC ebook record available at https://lccn.loc.gov/2022043093

ISBN: HB: 978-1-5013-8950-4
PB: 978-1-5013-8951-1
ePDF: 978-1-5013-8953-5
eBook: 978-1-5013-8952-8

Typeset by Deanta Global Publishing Services, Chennai, India
Printed and bound in Great Britain

Series: 33 1/3 Oceania

To find out more about our authors and books visit www.bloomsbury.com and sign up for our newsletters.

For Ben, Mia and Arlo

Contents

List of figures x
Acknowledgements xi

1   **Introduction** 1

2   **'Out on the Street': Space Waltz takes New Zealand by storm** 7

3   **What came before** 25

4   **The album part 1: *Space Waltz by Alastair Riddell* EMI (NZ) 1975** 33

5   **The album part 2** 61

6   **What came after** 97

Notes 111
Bibliography 120
Index 124

Figures

2.1   Advertisement for the 'Out on the Street' single, EMI
      1974 8

2.2   Space Waltz, Studio One/New Faces, 1 September
      1974 12

3.1   Alastair Riddell, Auckland Battle of the Bands, 1968 27

4.1   The full wrap-around cover image 40

Acknowledgements

My sincere thanks to Space Waltz – Alastair Riddell, Eddie Raynor, Brent Eccles, Greg Clark and Peter Cuddihy – for the inspiration you provided to me and to the rest of New Zealand's youth in 1974/75 and for your support in the creation of this book. My gratitude also goes to Alan Galbraith, Lisa Marr, Susan Videler and the School of Performing Arts, University of Otago, Dunedin, New Zealand.

1 Introduction

Alastair Riddell and Space Waltz shocked New Zealand to its core. When they burst into the nation's consciousness via the still relatively new but enormously popular medium of television, the nation was totally unprepared. Featuring with baffling incongruity on the light entertainment show, *Studio One/New Faces*, the five musicians, Alastair Riddell, Tony Raynor, Brent Eccles, Peter Cuddihy and Greg Clark, polarized the populace the length and breadth of the country. It was the beginning of a short but tumultuous career that would leave a telling and permanent mark upon the nation's social and popular music histories.

When the band's album, *Space Waltz by Alastair Riddell*, was released in 1975, rock music was the dominant force in youth culture. It was very, very important in a way that is hard to comprehend today, especially for those who weren't there. Literally tribal, one's music tastes spoke volumes, and an album held casually under the arm with front cover judiciously facing outwards positioned one in the eyes of others without a word spoken. Rock was a flagship behind which youth rallied en masse, aligning themselves to stylistic indicators bearing names such as prog (progressive), glam, metal and punk. To paraphrase football legend Bill Shankley, it wasn't a matter of life and death; it was much more serious than that. Intense debates over this or that song, album or act flourished in grimy and flashy suburbs alike, in schoolyards, at parties, on the factory floor and on university campuses as the aural art of the rock musician offered insightful, emotional and sometimes political commentaries on the world in a manner far more stimulating than the six o'clock news ever could. But even more tellingly, the ever-creative medium of rock had the potential to offer tantalizing glimpses of what might yet come to pass. The future. *Space Waltz by Alastair Riddell* offered this.

Today rock music finds itself just one option among many in the competition for youth attention and affiliation. The internet age offers an individualized smorgasbord of taste variations that can be minutely tweaked and tweaked again until all potential for widespread unification is lost. Gatekeeping algorithms ensure that nothing new or challenging is presented, multimedia options abound and gaming, cell phones, tablets, iPads and laptops encourage the privileging of vision over sound.

In 1975 it wasn't like that. Remember the experience of slipping a new 33 rpm record out of its sleeve and placing it carefully upon the turntable of your home stereo? Positioning headphones upon your ears, you'd settle back, close your eyes and the seductive warm crackle of needle settling into groove would draw you into a world very different to the one inhabited by your physical body. Ingress was through the ears, and excitement and possibility unfolded track by track. The imagery in your head was far more potent than any screen could ever offer because it was your own imagination filling in the gaps. Magic. In 1975 Aucklander Alastair Riddell and his fellow musicians created just such an alternative and futuristic world, and they invited young New Zealanders to join them. Many did so.

Of course, the album didn't come out of nowhere. Its remarkable back story involves an unlikely MOR television talent quest, a startling mimed performance of an outstanding original song called 'Out on the Street' that subsequently soared to the top of the New Zealand Singles Chart, and the resulting stardom, polarization, abhorrence and adoration. These preliminary events are, therefore, the subject of the opening chapter of this book.

The band's fortunes rose and fell spectacularly like no other New Zealand rock act before or since. Hot on the heels of their number-one hit single, they were awarded the coveted 'Best New Artist' award at the Recorded Arts Talent Awards (aka the RATAs) at the beginning of 1975. Nationwide tours followed along with a record deal with EMI that led to the solitary album addressed in this book. Yet within just two years, the Space Waltz journey would come to an abrupt end in nearby Australia in poverty, disagreement, disillusionment and disbanding. With dubious management decisions, rifts with record companies, tensions both within and outside the band, and other factors considered in this book, the Space Waltz story truly was one of rags-to-riches-to-rags.

As the author I cannot feign impartiality. I am a Space Waltz fan. The startling televisual moment that spawned their number-one hit remains crystal clear, finding me aged fourteen and sitting in the starkly lit communal kitchen/dining room of a cheap motor camp in Wellington, along with a group of fellow Boy's Brigade boys visiting from my hometown of Hamilton. We were in the capital city for a jamboree during the school holidays. With our camp leader in charge, we'd just finished dinner and were reluctantly surveying the dirty dishes with one eye on the telly that sat precariously high up on a shelf in a corner of the room. The nation's must-watch talent quest *Studio One/New Faces* was on. The room was full of other campers too – family groups and travellers. There was a steady hum of conversation, laughter and a rattling of dishes that challenged the audibility of the contestants. Well, at least that *was* the case until the words 'Watch out, young love' poured forth from Alastair Riddell's lips at the commencement of Space Waltz's performance. A hush fell upon the room, fully laden forks found their upwards trajectory stalled and from this point onwards the television was watched in silence, broken only occasionally by under-the-breath mutterings of deep discontent from various affronted adults for whom sleep would come slowly that night. Sleep would come slowly for me and legions of other kids around the country too, but for a very different reason. In Space Waltz and especially in lead singer Riddell, we had just caught a glimpse of the future. And we liked it.

Alastair Riddell and Space Waltz were gamechangers. Nevertheless, while their hit endures as part of the fabric of popular culture, their solitary album has received scant attention. I hope this book helps to rectify that.

There is little merit in being a copycat, but this was the oft-heard accusation hurled at Riddell in 1974 and 1975. This was the era of glam rock, and the king, David Bowie, was twelve thousand miles away. When Riddell and company mimed 'Out on the Street' to a nation held in thrall before their black-and-white TV sets by the band's radically different vision of Kiwi masculinity (especially Riddell), the nearest brickbats were accusations of copying England's androgynous Mr Bowie. The scared, the staid and the unimaginative duly reached for these and gleefully hurled them. Perhaps it was unsurprising. New Zealand had never seen the like; this land of black singlets and gumboots where, it was supposed, men could fix anything with a piece of no.8 wire and a stiff jaw as long as emotions were kept buried. Truly, Alastair Riddell single-handedly created a gender earthquake upon these shores, and, yes, there are parallels to be found with the shockwave that David Bowie had earlier created in the UK.

Another of my intentions is to challenge the all-too-easy copycat accusations that abounded and endured. Yes, Riddell was influenced by Bowie, and he's always been candid in acknowledging it. But who wasn't influenced by Bowie? To lazily write off Riddell as some kind of B-grade Bowie clone without bothering to go deeper is to overlook the myriad other thematic influences evident in his artistic palette. In addition – and perhaps most damagingly of all – the shockwave that his performance unleashed overshadowed and/or devalued his songwriting and performative prowess. For all the extraordinary merits of 'Out on the Street', it is on the album that these talents can best be found. Riddell's lyrics, in particular, are a feature of his songwriting that sets him apart, and I am grateful that he has allowed me to reproduce them in this book in order to provide the clearest and most direct gateway for the reader/listener into his extraordinary, highly literary world.

Another motivating factor is my desire to tackle the question of stylistic allegiance. Space Waltz is frequently all but written off in some quarters as (merely) 'a glam band' – a description that too often carries with it unwarranted inferences of shallowness and a lack of substance. I will argue that the album's true allegiance lies in progressive/art rock as much as glam.

Like the best artists in any field, Riddell and his band took influences from all over, absorbed/devoured them thoroughly, mixed them with their own ideas and then created something new and exciting. In mid-1970s New Zealand, Alastair Riddell and Space Waltz were exactly that: exciting, radical, challenging and trail-blazing. Above all they created art – New Zealand art – of a quality that deserves to be remembered, acknowledged and celebrated on its own merits and not, as has sometimes been the case, qualified and/or devalued by weary comparisons to overseas acts.

Finally, a note regarding my primary sources. It's been a pleasure to have the invaluable cooperation of all of the original band members: Alastair Riddell, Peter Cuddihy, Tony (Eddie) Raynor, Brent Eccles and Greg Clark. In addition, I am grateful for the recollections of the album's producer, Alan Galbraith. I should gently acknowledge, however, that our interactions have taken place almost fifty years after the fact. Understandably, memories fade, and therefore individual recollections occasionally bordered on contradictory. It's possible, therefore, that there may be some errors, although I hope, if so, that these will be both minor and few.

2 'Out on the Street'
Space Waltz takes
New Zealand by storm

Alastair Riddell and Space Waltz were overnight sensations and glam rock, in the svelte shape of 'Out on the Street', was here.[1]

'Out on the Street' made an indelible mark on New Zealand's popular culture (Figure 2.1). A number-one hit single in late 1974 – the first local number one in four years – it would go on to sit almost innocuously as the concluding track of side one of the album. Without this unique song and televisual phenomenon, *Space Waltz by Alastair Riddell* would likely never have seen the light of day.

Not only was 'Out on the Street' the high point of Riddell's career in terms of public acclaim, it underlined perfectly an observation made by Roger Jarrett in the editorial column of rock magazine *Hot Licks*. One month after Riddell's song topped the chart, Jarrett argued the case for a resurgence of the 45 rpm single:

Now is the time for the rebirth of singles as a viable sales item in your local record store. In times of tight money it makes just

Figure 2.1 *Advertisement for the 'Out on the Street' single, EMI 1974. Courtesy of Universal Music New Zealand.*

so much sense to offer a single at a reasonable price to induce the purchaser to buy a full price album. With a rebirth of singles, both on air and on the shelf, it would enable acts without company support to scrape together enough money to record a single and gain exposure. This is not worth attempting at the moment as singles are at such a low point unless there is other media involved. (e.g. Alastair Riddell and Space Waltz's television coverage of Out in the Streets [*sic*], a single that is approaching 5,000 sales – living proof that the medium can exist.)[2]

The combination of Riddell's extraordinary song and his audacious, in-the-face-of-the-nation performance in just such 'other media' – in this case, television talent quest *Studio One/ New Faces* – proved a perfect recipe for success.

Studio One/New Faces was so middle-of-the-road it straddled the white line in its brief to appeal to, but never offend, middle

New Zealand. Prior to 1974, the two components, *Studio One* and *New Faces*, had been separate light entertainment shows. *Studio One* was a competition for songwriters who could perform their songs themselves, if they were deemed to have sufficient talent, or have them performed by one of the nation's best-loved established singers. *New Faces* unveiled new performing talent never seen by the public. Indeed, it was a condition of entry that performers must never have appeared on television before.

In 1974's inaugural joining of the formats, thirty new songs and thirty new acts were put before a panel of four judges, the performances pre-recorded in front of a 'live' studio audience. Run over twelve weeks, each episode was split between three original songs and three new acts. At the conclusion of each performance, the judges would give their appraisals and award a mark out of twenty-five. Once completed the marks were tallied into an overall score, and those who scored the highest would progress to the final.

Screening on the country's only television channel, *Studio One* and *New Faces* had proven themselves invaluable as stepping-stones for artists, including songwriters Shona Laing, John Hanlon and Steve Allen, and performers such as The Rumour, Hogsnort Rupert, Anna Leah, Steve Gilpin and Suzanne Prentice. With no other means of gaining such invaluable exposure, now and then a rock band would bravely take the stage. They did so knowing it was a very long way from their natural environment but nevertheless treated it as a somewhat awkward but worthy means to an end. In 1994, musicologists Bruce Sheridan and Philip Hayward looked back at *Studio One/New Faces* and observed, 'Despite their potential to generate sublime (or ridiculous) contrasts, such shows were not particularly conducive showcases for the style(s) of more "serious", often album-oriented, rock music which emerged in the 1970s.[3] Author and historian Chris Bourke recalls, 'The occasional rock band would awkwardly appear beside barbershop Quartets and boy Sopranos.'[4] The most notable of these rock bands was Split Enz (then called Split Ends), who competed in 1973, the year before Space Waltz. As bassist Mike Chunn observes, '*New Faces* was going to allow us the chance to go up against the fire-eaters, folkies and comedy acts.'[5] Chunn elaborated further regarding Split Enz's motivation, recalling that the preceding 1972 competition had aroused the band's interest:

> The New Faces talent quest had national attention. In those days, the only television channel was a government department and was able to spend exorbitant amounts of money flying contestants from all around New Zealand to mime out heats in their Wellington studios. The year before, two of the finalists, John Hanlon and Shona Laing, had gone on to fairly substantial careers with top 10 records as a result of the exposure they had received from the series.[6]

In 1973 Split Ends progressed through their heat and contested the final, won by a novelty act from Wellington called Bulldog's Allstar Goodtime Band, who sported a washboard, kazoos, funny costumes and a tea chest bass. Middle New Zealand and the judges thrilled to their winking bonhomie. Judge Phil Warren, while acknowledging the obvious promise of Split Ends, ultimately summed up the true nature/level of the show by declaring Chunn and company 'too clever'. Nevertheless, the nationwide exposure was an enormous boon for the band. As Sheridan and Hayward noted, 'Rising acts gained valuable exposure by simply participating, whatever the jury's opinion of their worth.'[7]

This exposure was precisely why Space Waltz followed suit in 1974. As Riddell puts it, 'Studio One/New Faces was watched by nearly everybody in its seven o'clock slot on a Sunday evening.'[8] With 'Out on the Street' being an original song and Space Waltz being a new act, they could have appeared in either part of the show. In the event, they were placed in *New Faces*.

Space Waltz appeared as the final act of the second episode, screening on 1 September. Opening the show was Desna Sisarich performing a playful tongue-in-cheek Simon Morris and Al Park composition titled 'Boom Boom'. Frothy pop singer and family favourite Steve Allen followed with a schmaltzy original composition titled 'Storybook Love Affair'. Rounding out the *Studio One* part of the programme was the equally popular vocalist Annie Whittle, singing a gaze-at-the-stars ballad 'The Love I Feel', written by Jeanette Potts. First up in *New Faces* was the bearded Waiheke Island folkie Grant Goodwin, ill at ease in a smart suit, with his bouncy 'Spring Song' delivered with perfect articulation through a smile that wouldn't quit. Soprano Wiki Baker came next, singing Simon and Garfunkel's 'Bridge over Troubled Water', beautiful and saccharine. Then, in a juxtaposition that perfectly exemplified the show's wildly disparate nature, presenter Craig Little announced: 'And now for something completely different. It's a group from Auckland. They're called Space Waltz. They're a fulltime band, and they're

Figure 2.2 *Space Waltz*, Studio One/New Faces, *1 September 1974. Courtesy of Alastair Riddell.*

doing an original composition written by the lead singer in the group, Alastair Riddell. And it's called, "Out in [*sic*] the Street'".

Bang! Nothing would ever be the same (Figure 2.2).

The stage came into focus with the band members starkly backlit for a few seconds as Riddell's now iconic opening line, 'Watch out, young love', rang out across the studio and through the living rooms of New Zealand. At the last word, of that warning to the nation's youth, 'love', the spotlights revealed Alastair Riddell and Space Waltz to the nation for the first time. To say they were a revelation is inadequate. Speaking from my own experience of that moment, the nice-enough-but-is-this-all-there-is? New Zealand that I had always known was blown apart. With eyes like saucers, I drank in the wildly expanded blueprint for Kiwi masculinity that Riddell handed to the nation's youth. In that moment, aspiring to play rugby for the All Blacks was obliterated as a compulsory component in the rite of passage to adulthood for New Zealand boys. How about being a rock star instead? See? It *is* possible! 'Watch out, young love' indeed.

No home-grown musician had ever performed with such blatant chutzpah. Resplendent in platform shoes, silk trousers, scarf, satin jacket, mascara and lipstick, Riddell pouted and strode, strutted and posed. All the while he ate up the cameras like he'd been doing it for years – like he was a bona fide, long-established, international star. His direct unflinching eye contact gave him a powerful presence inside family homes the length and breadth of New Zealand. Laser-like, he could pin us to the floor. He was the star that came to dinner – completely uninvited. Never mind that the footage was black and white – his performance far transcended any such limitation. While adults ground their teeth, gripping their early evening cups of tea unnecessarily tightly as they willed the performance to end, the nation's children sat transfixed. As Riddell himself would later put it,

> The adults and the parents were shocked and appalled. They were shocked by this sexually ambiguous thing – this image – that came on their screens that was very powerful and all the kids thought it was fantastic! All the younger people thought it was amazing . . . and it had a polarizing effect. The record company and radio and television got 'Shocked mum of Tawa' letters for some time after that.[9]

Unsurprisingly, given the gift to ratings provided by the band's peacock-like lead singer/guitarist, glimpses of the other musicians were fleeting. But all four took Riddell's lead in terms of miming with confidence and attitude.

As the band was raising eyebrows and temperatures with their image and Riddell's assured, even arrogant stage manner, their sound was matching that visual impact, their collective musical talent shining through. Wade Ronald Churton remembers, 'Riddell pouting, posing, stage-gasping and camping it up a la Bowie and Bolan, over some dramatic, hard pop-rock.'[10]

The sheer compositional class of 'Out on the Street' as a hit-in-waiting was clear. Riddell's obvious literary bent and clever mastery of language conjured up mental images of another world. 'A sign of Aphrodite?' 'A grave apocalypse? Even the vocal manner with which Riddell put across his song broke new ground. Never had a New Zealand rock singer adopted such an affected and theatrical singing style.

In short, 'Out on the Street' hit the country with a dose of dangerous shock-of-the-new. The small, inoffensive nation at the bottom of the world had never experienced anything like it and the following recollections typify the impact upon the nation's youth. Kiwi music legend Don McGlashan (ex-Blam Blam Blam, The Front Lawn, Muttonbirds), then fifteen years old, recalls, 'We'd just had dinner and the house was filled with the smell of cabbage and corned beef and we got the impression that nothing was ever going to change. And then, all of a sudden, everything was different!'[11] Music writer Grant Smithies recounts:

It was one of those alarming 'What the fuck . . .!' moments where you find yourself instantly understanding something on one level, and being profoundly bewildered by it on another. Physically, I felt as though the walls of my parent's already teensy Wanganui living-room had come rushing in at me. Emotionally, it felt like a Grand Canyon-sized chasm had just opened up between me and anyone who did not 'get' this song. My parents hated 'Out on the Street' immediately . . . which naturally fanned the flames of my ardour. It was a clear case of 'Oops – there goes the neighbourhood!'[12]

Fellow music writer Nick Bollinger too recalls the moment's transformative nature:

Like most New Zealanders, my first encounter with Alastair Riddell was in my own living room, in black and white. The tall androgynous figure with dark tresses, silver eye shadow and white satin bell-bottoms, with a scarf trailing almost to the floor, pouted and preened his way through a song that seemed to be an ode to a drag queen. His appearance caused visible discomfort among the all-male judging panel. Space Waltz represented, if not quite the end of the world . . . then a distinct alternative.[13]

Music reviewer and blogger Gary Steel reflects:

Dad probably made the obligatory comment that they looked like poofs, but he thought all longhairs were poofs, regardless of rouge or eye shadow. I had the trusty National portable cassette recorder placed as close to the tinny speaker of our black and white TV as possible to catch the musical goodness. As I had done the year before with Split Enz, I was beside myself with parochial pride at the sight of Alastair and pals proving that Kiwi music was strong enough to take its place on the world stage. Long, flowing hair. Incredible song. From my adolescent living room, the scent was a pheromonic attractant that simply could not be denied. Out on the streets! If only! Hamilton's streets hardly seemed worth being out on. The song held out the irresistible promise of revolution and transgression: sexual, societal, whatever. My 15-year-old self was transfixed.[14]

Simon Grigg, ex-Suburban Reptiles, founder of Propeller Records, rock journalist, band manager and music historian, also has the moment etched in his memory:

> Like most teenagers in New Zealand with the television switched on, on that fateful night in 1974 – and, really, there was little else to do in those slightly grey days – I was enthralled/excited and a little shocked by the unexpected arrival of Alastair Riddell and his group Space Waltz on our screens. David Bowie was one thing, a secret thing the kids didn't feel the need to tell the adults about, and he was over there. But here was ours, on prime time TV, and it was a far more androgynous and challenging variant. That opening cry of 'Watch out, young love' was our Bill Grundy moment and the exact moment when the sixties finally died in New Zealand. Within a few months, Riddell was filling the Auckland Town Hall on a winter's Monday night. The future had arrived.[15]

Back to Earth.

After the performance ended to enthusiastic applause from the studio audience – younger members beaming ear to ear – presenter Craig Little sported a wry smile as he back-announced the act: 'The group was called Space Waltz, the song, "Out in [*sic*] the Street". Some mixed reactions to that, I think!', he quipped, before turning to the judges.

The judges were an interesting mix. Two decades later, musicologists Sheridan and Hayward would observe of *Studio One/New Faces* judges across the various seasons: 'The show's panel of judges included promoters and performers and was often marked by heated discussion and fluctuating taste-based criteria.'[16] The judging panel of 1974 aligned closely to this observation.

In an article in the *New Zealand Listener* magazine published a week before the series started, the judges were profiled. Nick Karavias, selected for his experience in the recording industry, was described as an employee of record company HMV, having initially been the company's stock controller before moving into a creative role as a record producer.[17] Karavias, the article further noted, had been on the *Studio One* judging panel once previously. Paddy O'Donnell had also been employed in the role in a previous season of *Studio One*, bringing radio and television experience to the panel. O'Donnell had worked on the television show *Town and Around* and filled a variety of roles in radio stations throughout New Zealand and Australia. Howard Morrison was a household name in the local entertainment industry, having worked nationally and internationally as a highly successful solo entertainer since 1964 after disbanding the equally popular Māori showband, the Howard Morrison Quartet. The fourth judge on the 1974 panel was Phil Warren, returning for a third stint in the role; he was well known to the public. Warren's wide industry experience included being the managing director of Prestige Promotions and Prestige Cabarets Limited, a company that ran nightclubs.

When Craig Little opened the floor to the judges at the conclusion of Space Waltz's performance, confused and argumentative opinions were expressed. Frequent interruptions occurred, eyes were rolled and brows furrowed, mock kisses were blown and eyelashes batted provocatively (Morrison), betraying 1970s-style homophobia. At times voices were raised. It was clear Space Waltz had presented the judges with something well outside their expectations. Nonetheless, the obvious quality of the song, the enthusiastic audience reaction and the professionalism of the act held sway. Interruptions and asides excluded, the judges' comments were as follows:

Nick Karavias: 'A splendid example of what I would call obnoxious rock. I must admit that, though it's not to my taste, I think they are very professional and they're doing their thing in great style.'

Paddy O'Donnell: 'I don't know that the David Bowie thing isn't overdone now, but notwithstanding, this effeminate thing is very commercial in the heavy area. I thought they had a ton of showmanship. But I think, lyric-wise, listening to the song – I enjoyed the song – I think it would be G-string rating.'

Howard Morrison: 'To each his own as far as taste of music is concerned. I give top marks for the effort in writing about a very difficult subject, and I give full marks to the presentation. Um, in its capacity, very well done.'

Phil Warren: 'Great TV potential. Very now. I would say the biggest selling record in the country at the moment is *Diamond Dogs* with Bowie, so they are very now. Not overdone with the makeup, great impact, potential, originality, their own song, the grooming was fine. I think they've got a great future.'

The scores awarded by the judges at the conclusion of their appraisals were:

Nick Karavias: 19
Paddy O'Donnell: 19
Howard Morrison: 17
Phil Warren: 18

The resulting seventy-three points left Space Waltz as runners-up behind Wiki Baker (seventy-four) but ahead of Grant Goodwin (sixty-eight), therefore propelling them through to the final.

Becoming a finalist carried benefits beyond qualification. Every show concluded with a recap of all finalists, thus a valuable few seconds of 'Out on the Street' served as a weekly reminder of the song to the nation. As Riddell recalls, 'A portion of the performance was played at the end of each week's show. So "Out on the Street" was there making its huge impression on the New Zealand public every week.'[18] Given that Space Waltz qualified in just the second week of twelve, this was extremely significant.

The effect that this exposure had on Riddell personally was considerable. He relates:

It was a heady and a weird and wonderful time, and I often found it difficult to deal with. Even a trip to the supermarket was impossible without feeling self-conscious. I was 6'4" tall, with hair halfway down my back . . . it was hard to be inconspicuous. Heads would crane over shelves or around aisle ends. I got sick of that in the end, and for a while I didn't want to go out.[19]

And so to the final. The rules required that acts recorded and mimed a different song. 'Beautiful Boy', another song that would feature on the upcoming album, was chosen. Performing seven of eight acts and with Split Enz bassist Mike Chunn standing in for the unavailable Peter Cuddihy, the band was introduced by presenter Craig Little, who noted that 'Space Waltz was one of the acts that brought the most comments from people young and old during the earlier part of the series'.

Once again led by Riddell's visual flamboyance and received enthusiastically by the audience, they nevertheless failed to impress the judges to the same degree. A very complex song, with lyrics both sung and spoken at times, 'Beautiful Boy' lacked the obvious pop credentials of 'Out on the Street'. It proved much more difficult for Riddell to mime to. The decision to even attempt to mime such a complex piece drew praise from Warren, while Karavias openly criticized Riddell for it. 'Now that's unfair!' retorted Warren, adding, 'Naughty, naughty' towards his fellow judge. Inconsistencies underlined the panel's appraisal again, with much interjecting and arguing.

Nick Karavias: 'I can only say they've maintained the high quality of presentation and musicianship of their first showing. The only reservation I have is . . . the lack of versatility and the fact that they only appeal to a thinnish segment of the population. A lot of people probably don't like them.'

Howard Morrison: 'I will say this and say this only. On their first performance, this is not up to it. And I expected more.'

Phil Warren: 'That was a very difficult number you did, and to mime that . . . top marks. Guts! I think the first thing you recorded, "Out on the Street" . . . that's gonna be a hit for you. I really do. . . . I like you. I like you very much!'

Paddy O'Donnell: 'I was hoping you'd do something different second time around to give us, the judges, a chance to look at what else you can deliver. You're very stylised on those two performances and that limits your appeal. Now I'm not saying you're no good. But [for] TV performances, you need a lot of ideas, fellahs. And television chews up performers and spits them out. I thought you may have been used up in those two performances. But I'm very glad you made the finals.'

With the judges' comments made, each awarded Space Waltz a score as follows:

Paddy O'Donnell: 16
Nick Karavias: 23
Phil Warren: 22
Howard Morrison: 21

When O'Donnell's low score of sixteen points appeared on the scoreboard, it was met with loud displeasure from the audience and even his fellow judges, Warren in particular. Ultimately, Space Waltz finished sixth.

Studio One/New Faces 1974: Final Scores (in order of performance)

Graham Sherlock and the Walker Family 89
Wiki Baker 77
Distillery 81
Davina Henderson 86
Rhys Kirk and Friends 90

Lauren Havill 95

Space Waltz 82

The Hammond Family 91

Success in the final was not particularly important, and, in truth, due to their obvious square-peg-in-a-round-hole nature, they could never have won. As Riddell himself has said, it was still 'mission accomplished'.[20] Space Waltz was now a household name. And in the same week that the final was broadcast, 'Out on the Street' hit number one on the New Zealand Singles Chart because Alan Galbraith, EMI house producer and head of local A&R, had purchased the master tape of the song from the New Zealand Broadcasting Corporation (NZBC) so that it could be remastered and rush-released.

Even before their television debut went to air, Galbraith had his eye upon them. The producer of *Studio One/New Faces*, Chris Bourne, had been so impressed by the live audition he'd seen in the NZBC Theatre in Auckland that he played the tape to EMI's main man. Suitably impressed, Galbraith had immediately contacted Riddell with the offer of a record contract. Notably, the deal was for Riddell alone, not the entire band. Galbraith regarded Alastair Riddell and Space Waltz as something special. In his own recent words to this author, 'What appealed to me was that they had the whole package – great song, well played, and Alastair had a great presence on screen, pure star quality.'[21]

Riddell recalls that the band's audition tape didn't include 'Out on the Street', but he proffered it after being accepted. 'We actually ambushed them. "Out on the Street" wasn't even the song we did for the audition. But then we went down to Wellington and said "This is the song we think we should do" and Chris Bourne said "Alright!"'[22]

Dr Graeme Downes, music academic, 1980s rock star and front-man for Dunedin's indie legends The Verlaines, sums up the ultimate against-the-odds triumph of Riddell and Space Waltz:

> I remember at the time the supreme vindication of the song becoming No 1 after the fatuous Phil Warren et al (entertainment managers or had-been entertainers from Auckland who were the judges) didn't even place the band in the top three of the final. I remember the scowling face of Mister Riddell conveying an unmistakable regret at ever having maintained the notion that prostituting his band and song writing talent on a TV talent show was a good idea. I felt a small thrill of vindication that my taste and that of young NZer's had given the older generation something of a black eye, at least as far as their narrow definition of what constituted 'entertainment' was concerned.[23]

With his hit single, extensive youth fanbase and instant nationwide star status, Riddell's hastily arranged contract with EMI extended to a full album, with recording beginning just two months later. 'Out on the Street' was seemingly just the beginning of even greater things to come. Riddell remembers:

> 'Out on the Street' was hugely successful because young people loved the fact that it was challenging to their parents. In a vicarious way it was exciting and daring for a socially

conservative country like New Zealand of the time. It seemed to drag us kicking and screaming into the modern world.[24]

The younger members of New Zealand's 'modern world' wanted more of Alastair Riddell and Space Waltz; this band that had come out of nowhere and shredded the normally dubious connotations of the word 'local'. A full album? Bring it on!

3 What came before

Space Waltz may well have seemingly come out of nowhere, but the seeds had been sown many years before.

Alastair Riddell was born in Auckland in 1952 and spent his childhood in Titirangi, a bush-clad suburb in the Waitakere Ranges. Growing up in a house filled with visual art, books and intellectual discussion, with musically talented parents and creatively inclined family friends and acquaintances, Alastair's artistic and academic leanings were cultivated early. It wasn't so much whether his future lay in the arts but more which one he would adopt.

At eight he began lessons in classical piano and began to teach himself to play the guitar. With a natural aptitude and ability to play by ear and from notation, from this point the die was cast. His older brother Ron had taken up the drums, and when their parents bought Alastair an electric guitar for his twelfth birthday, the two began to jam. In June 1964 when the Beatles played at the Auckland Town Hall, Alastair was there and his fate was sealed.

While in the fourth form at Kelston Boy's High School, Alastair formed a band with friend and future Space Waltz bassist Peter Cuddihy. Outside school that year and despite his relative youth, he joined a bluesy rock band called The Original Sun Blues Band. Founded by local blues guitar aficionado Henry Jackson, the name paid homage to blues icon Son

House. The band featured Alastair's brother Ron on drums; legend has it that the other members were unaware that their new recruit was so young because of his extraordinary height. This notion lasted until the Riddells' mother instructed them one night that Alastair was not to be kept out late as he had to get up for school the next morning.

Music historian Roger Watkins, an expert on the Auckland scene of the 1960s, describes the band:

> Their music was American blues as opposed to English blues a la Mayall. They gigged on the university circuit, at the Montemarte on blues nights, the Limehouse Blues Club and the Wynard Arms Coffee House. For a year they steadfastly played their covers of Buddy Guy, Muddy Waters, Elmore James, John Lee Hooker, Albert and B.B. King songs to the core of dedicated blues fans in the vangard of the blues scene in Auckland. On odd occasions when they ventured into the nightclub scene, they found their repertoire was too obscure for most patrons. Invariably there were arguments with management over the material they insisted on performing.[1]

Musical disagreements found the Riddells and other band members going their separate ways, and left in the brothers' hands, the name was truncated to Original Sun. With a changed repertoire, including covers of Jimi Hendrix and Cream plus original songs, into the fold came Alastair's friend Peter Cuddihy. Forging ahead as a three piece and confining their activities to the university circuit, Original Sun also contested Auckland's popular Battle of the Bands in 1968 and 1969 (Figure 3.1).

Figure 3.1 *Alastair Riddell, Auckland Battle of the Bands, 1968. Courtesy of Alastair Riddell.*

In 1968 the entrepreneurial Alastair organized New Zealand's first-ever Blues Convention, held at Moller's Farm in Oratia, West Auckland. Besotted with music, he started a newsletter called *Bluesnews*.

The beginning of the 1970s found Alastair undertaking a degree in anthropology at the University of Auckland. In 1971, Peter Cuddihy introduced him to two like-minded musicians in keyboard player Tony (aka Eddie) Raynor and drummer Paul Crowther. They jointly decided to form a new band, recruiting guitarist Paul (Wally) Wilkinson, and the group was christened Orb. Retaining their university origins and true to their progressive rock bent – Riddell was even playing a

synthesizer, the rarest of beasts at the time, built by Crowther
– they gathered a small enthusiastic student fanbase with
their mix of King Crimson, David Bowie, Genesis and Yes
covers and a growing repertoire of originals. Of particular
note was the lengthy and complex 'Seabird', a Riddell-penned
song that would later feature on the Space Waltz album –
early evidence of the compositional sophistication of which
he was capable. By this point rock music had become an
obsession for Riddell: 'Getting towards my late teens . . . I got
completely distracted, left university and became obsessed
with being a rock'n'roll star.'[2]

In 1973 Orb gave a well-received performance at the
Ngāruawāhia Music festival, a now-legendary event in
local music history. This first-ever outdoor festival featured
a stellar line-up of currently hot and/or up-and-coming
international and national acts, including Black Sabbath,
Fairport Convention, Blerta, The La De Das, Split Ends (Enz),
Max Merrit & the Meteors, Bulldog's Allstar Goodtime Band,
Corben Simpson, Billy TK's Powerhouse, Mammal and the
nascent Dragon.

Riddell and Raynor in particular had confidence in the
band's potential, Riddell even recalling an ambitious proposal
to relocate to the UK. This level of confidence was not shared
by the others, however; and Ngāruawāhia was to be their
swansong. Remarkably, no fewer than three members would
later reunite in Split Ends/Enz: Eddie Raynor, Paul (Wally)
Wilkinson and Paul Crowther.

In 1973 a young Auckland drummer, Brent Eccles, sought
musicians to form a touring covers band on the financially
lucrative, if artistically stifling, breweries circuit. As he recalls,

Lion Breweries were crying out for bands . . . I began placing ads in the major Auckland newspapers for musicians for $100 per week each. For this time $100 was particularly good money. This was born out by the massive number of replies I had. Just about every available musician in Auckland must have answered the call. It was mind boggling and I didn't really know where to start.[3]

Opting to proceed without holding auditions, Eccles and bassist Cuddihy instead approached musicians they knew of personally. Guitarist Greg Clark was invited to join but politely declined as his day job meant he could not tour. Cuddihy then suggested Alastair Riddell for the guitar role. As Eccles further recollects,

It sounded OK to me so we went round to Alastair's house and put it to him. Alastair was working in his garage on a VW at the time so we had most of the conversation by talking under the jacked up vehicle to this manly, well-spoken chap. He was really keen and doubly so if we were to also attract a keyboard player called Tony Raynor who was in his last band, Orb.[4]

Raynor too was keen, and in the Riddell family's garage a new band, Stewart & the Belmonts, began to rehearse a repertoire of pub-friendly covers. While this was not what they ultimately aspired to and with Riddell by now putting considerable effort into writing originals, they all recognized the value in the opportunity. Riddell says:

All of us wanted to do original music, but it was a great way of learning your essentials of being a good musician. One of the great things about the pub network and the booze barns in those days was, as a young musician, you could earn a living and you could travel around the country and learn your trade.[5]

Regarding the band's unusual name, suggested by friend Rick Styles, Riddell recalls,

It was a bit of a throwaway drug allusion because Brian Stewart was the head of the drug squad in Auckland and they drove Holden Belmonts. It was a bit obtuse, but I think some people got the joke. . . . Sometimes people would come up to us when we were playing and say, 'Which one of you is Stewart?' and we'd swap around and all take turns.[6]

Riddell, Eccles, Raynor and Cuddihy debuted on the breweries circuit with a week at the local pub in the Waikato timber town of Kawerau, performing as a band in their own right but also backing guest artists. They did well and their contract was extended to a month. Upon returning to Auckland, however, they discovered their agent had fallen out with the brewery's booker of bands. As a result, while they went ahead with their next confirmed booking at the Trees Tavern in Tokoroa, work dried up. Needing more income than the band could provide, Raynor left to join another, Cruise Lane; Cuddihy found work with a three-piece act in a restaurant, while Eccles became a postman.

Shortly after this Riddell purchased his own house in Auckland, into which he moved with his then wife, Cilla. Cuddihy and his girlfriend, Angie, joined them, along with Eccles, who takes up the story: 'Out in the back yard was an old tool shed which Peter, Alastair and I converted into a rehearsal room. We'd work as a three piece on Alastair's songs when Peter had free time.'[7]

Riddell and Eccles decided to resurrect Stewart and the Belmonts as a money-making venture. With Cuddihy unavailable, bassist Steve Hughes joined along with his friend vocalist Steve Kielly, and guitarist Greg Clark. Raynor, now available again, re-joined. Working for the well-known Fuller's Entertainment Bureau, the band accepted every gig they were offered, including weddings, socials, twenty-first birthday parties, events on military bases and school dances. As Eccles recalls, 'Our motto was "We're only in it for the money", which meant we could easily justify playing anywhere.'[8]

Hearing that auditions were imminent for 1974's *Studio One/ New Faces*, Riddell, Eccles, Cuddihy, Clark and Raynor decided that the show would be a useful vehicle for trying out Riddell's original songs on the public, also noting the exposure secured by Split Ends the year before. Once a new name was decided – Stewart and the Belmonts was not considered given the very different aims and styles of the two ventures – Eccles cut out the entry form from the *New Zealand Listener*, filled it out and posted it away. The band's name on the entry form was Space Waltz, the result of a brainstorming session Riddell and Eccles had undertaken in Riddell's dining room during which they'd written science fiction and dance-related words on pieces of paper and swapped them around. When eventually Space Waltz came up, Riddell exclaimed, 'That's it! That's the one! That's fantastic!'[9]

Space Waltz auditioned at Auckland's NZBC Theatre. Two original songs and two tracks from David Bowie's recently released *Pinups* album were chosen for the occasion; however, the audition almost never happened because Eccles' van, loaded with the band's gear, would not start. Seen as a bad omen they almost abandoned the audition, until Eccles rang his father in a last effort to get help. Mr Eccles arrived and, remarkably, towed the fully laden van to the audition.

With *Studio One/New Faces* producer Chris Bourne in attendance, things went well, and Bourne informed the band on the spot that they would be accepted for a place in the heats. Sure enough a letter of confirmation arrived, and the band found themselves booked to fly to Wellington.

Having decided that 'Out on the Street' would be their best shot at progressing, the band recorded the song at Wellington's NZBC recording studio on the same day as their television appearance that evening. Although time was tight, they'd rehearsed thoroughly and were delighted at how the track came together. Once done, the band was summoned to their make-up call at the TV studio. As Eccles remembers, 'We had decided to go for a glam rock appearance which meant a pretty full make up job, so wandering round the TV studio in full camp regalia sent a few ripples through the place.'[10]

With the musicians ready, the audience seated and the judges and presenter Craig Little in position, the cameras began to roll for heat two of *Studio One/New Faces* 1974.

And the rest, as they say, is history.

NB: During the months between their heat and the final, the band faced the unusual situation of continuing to be booked by their agency for gigs as Stewart and the Belmonts. Eccles recalls, '[They] had this annoying habit of booking Stewart and the Belmonts into gigs and telling people that we were really Space Waltz. When we got to the gigs the guests would be primed for us to play "Out on the Street" and do the whole bit, but we never did.'[11]

4 The album part 1
Space Waltz by Alastair Riddell
EMI (NZ) 1975

Side 1

Fräulein Love	3.50
Beautiful Boy	4.51
Seabird	8.40
Out on the Street	3.20

Side 2

Angel	3.56
Open Up	5.26
Scars of Love	3.28
And up to Now	3.37
Love the Way He Smiles	8.08

Credits

Alastair Riddell: Electric Guitar/Acoustic Guitar/Synthesizer/
  Arrangements/Vocals

Tony Raynor: Piano/Hammond Organ/ Mellotron/Synthesizer/
    Arrangements
Greg Clark: Electric Guitar
Peter Cuddihy: Bass Guitar
Brent Eccles: Drums
The Yandall Sisters: Vocal Backings
Alan Galbraith: A.R.P. Synthesizer/Vocal Backing

All selections written by Alastair Riddell. Published by EMI
    Music (A division of EMI (New Zealand) Limited).

Engineered at EMI Studios, Wellington by Michael
    Grafton-Green
Remix by Michael Grafton-Green and Alan Galbraith
Produced by Alan Galbraith
Photographs: Michael Baigent
Cover Design: Tony Aspland

Producer

Alan Galbraith, born in Luton, England, but raised in Nelson, New Zealand, spent his later childhood and early adulthood in the pursuit of pop stardom. Playing in a variety of bands in Nelson and Wellington and embarking upon a solo career, he was a talented guitarist, vocalist and musical all-rounder. When popular Palmerston North band Sounds Unlimited lost their lead singer – soon-to-be pop star Mr Lee Grant (aka Bogdan Kominowski) – Galbraith replaced him. Remaining with the band throughout 1966, he left in mid-1967 after a stint performing in the UK in order to form a duo, The Real

Thing, with Aucklander Ken Murphy. Although signed to HMV, the endeavour was short-lived as Galbraith was hospitalized with a kidney infection. It was during his lengthy recovery that he decided to become a record producer.

Following an initial position as producer and partner in Independent Record Productions (later renamed Direction Records), Galbraith accepted a position at HMV as an all-rounder. He says, 'I soon spent every available moment working in the studio as a musician, singer, composer – whatever was required, with or without pay. I would have scrubbed the floors if that's what it took. I soon got to see how it was all done.'[1]

In 1970 the workload falling upon HMV's star producer Peter Dawkins was such that a second producer was required, and Galbraith got his chance. Among his early credits were Brendon Dugan, The Kal-Q-Lated Risk, Highway, Tamburlaine and fourteen-year-old sensation David Curtis.

Songwriting success came Galbraith's way in 1971 via TV's *Studio One*, three years before it was combined with *New Faces*. Converting one of his poems, 'The Old Man', into a song, he was awarded joint first prize.

In June 1972 HMV was renamed EMI (NZ), and the roles of its two producers were expanded to include Artist and Repertoire. That is, they could sign and record whoever they wanted to. Galbraith states:

I was interested in creating hit records. Full stop. I guess I thought . . . I was the person with my finger on the pulse in terms of what the radio listeners wanted to hear and what the band could do . . . you're the catalyst; you're the bridge between one and the other.[2]

However, despite this perceived freedom, Dawkins and Galbraith became unhappy with the conservative approach of their employers and their poor salaries, and in 1972 both departed. Dawkins left for Australia and Galbraith for Britain, the latter working as a musician on a P&O liner.

Galbraith found employment with EMI (UK), working with independent producers, including the renowned Mickie Most, of Animals and Jeff Beck fame, who was at the time riding a wave of success with Suzi Quatro. Galbraith also worked with Deep Purple's label, Purple Records and tried unsuccessfully to convince EMI to sign the still unknown future giants Queen.

Although he was not long in the UK, the experience left a lasting impression. Galbraith realized that he was

> more comfortable when I could find the artist, choose the material, do the arrangements . . . I was the type of producer who said, 'I'm here to make pop records, you know.' And a bit of that I learned in London when I worked with RAK Records and saw what Most used to do with his people.[3]

Returning to New Zealand in early 1973, EMI and Galbraith repaired their relationship and he resumed his role. He reflects:

> My self-imposed mission was to build a stable of artists that could work together in the studio as well as live on stage, to foster some songwriting talent, and start building what I called 'New Zealand music to the world.' The concept was loosely based on the Stax Records model in the USA . . . Armed with a dangerous amount of new knowledge, I was more determined than ever to shake some trees.[4]

It was to be a notable return and a golden year, with major successes achieved with acts including Craig Scott, Link, Quincy Conserve and the highly eclectic Corben Simpson. In the near future Galbraith would exceed these successes by signing and/or recording acts such as Mark Williams, Sharon O'Neil and Rockinghorse. He would earn many awards, including Producer of the Year in 1975 and 1976, in acknowledgement of becoming one of the country's finest home-grown producers.

As 1973 rolled over into 1974, it was evident that Galbraith was fast establishing himself as the hit-maker he'd set out to be. On the lookout for unique New Zealand talent, Alastair Riddell and Space Waltz were just around the corner.

Engineer

Englishman Michael Grafton-Green spent twelve years at Abbey Road Studios in London before moving to New Zealand in 1969 to take up a position at the HMV Studio in Wellington. At Abbey Road he was a tape operator, second engineer and disc cutter, working with artists including the Beatles, Cliff Richard and The Shadows, The Hollies, Cilla Black and Shirley Bassey. While classical music was his first love, the work he'd undertaken with these artists must have proved inspiring to those he would work with in New Zealand. Upon arrival in Wellington, however, he found to his dismay that the studio was poorly equipped, so he appealed to EMI in London for an upgrade, subsequently taking delivery of a large Neve mixing desk and an eight-track recorder that had the capacity to be upgraded to sixteen tracks. After personally helping to assemble the new equipment, in the years that followed he would work with many New Zealand music icons, including Annah Leah, BLERTA, Allison Durbin, Quincy Conserve, Lutha, Rockinghorse, Ebony and Mark Williams. In an interview broadcast in 2013, just a year before his death, Grafton-Greene fondly recounted his experience of working with Riddell:

> He was amazing. I mean he got some amazing sounds out of that band. He came down from Auckland and it was really quite stunning. [It was] very exciting working with them. Alan Galbraith was the producer . . . and we worked well with him, getting the sound they wanted.[5]

Backing singers

New Zealand-born Samoan siblings, the Yandall Sisters were a popular act in their own right as well as being sought-after backing vocalists utilized by many top acts. The group members were Caroline, Mary, Adele and Pauline, although it was the latter three who would become the mainstay after Caroline moved to Australia. Among many achievements, they reached the top ten in 1975 (peaking at #8) with their version of 'Sweet Inspiration', a top twenty hit for the Sweet Inspirations in the United States in 1968. They were named New Zealand Entertainers of the Year in 1977, and in 2007 they received the Pacific Music Lifetime Achievement Award.

Once Riddell and the other musicians had completed recording the album tracks and with a basic mix achieved, the Yandall Sisters were summoned. This was something that occurred on many occasions during the mid-1970s. As Galbraith remembers,

> The Yandall Sisters were a major part of my session crew in the 70s and I would have brought them in after the main recording was completed. They picked up parts easily, were extremely versatile and very quick in the studio. They had that magical blend that you only get from siblings. They were real pros and I always loved working with them.[6]

Riddell recalls, 'I would sing lines that I thought might work, but the Yandalls, of course, were much more au fait with harmonies. Alan was quite experienced with them too, so between the three of us we hacked them out. I was really pleased with how it sounded.'[7]

The album cover

Photographs

Christchurch-born Michael Baigent was a friend of Riddell's during the early to mid-1970s. The two would engage in deep debates that pitted widely held and often unchallenged religious beliefs against historical fact. Such was Baigent's passion for the subject that, after moving to London in 1976, he established himself as a leading authority, producing no fewer than fourteen books that critiqued different aspects of Christianity. The most successful of these was *The Holy Blood and the Holy Grail* (1982). Co-authored by Richard Leigh and

Figure 4.1 *The full wrap-around cover image. Courtesy of Alastair Riddell.*

Henry Lincoln, the title became an international bestseller. Two decades later, when author Dan Brown wrote a novel with a similar theme, *The Da Vinci Code* (2003), Baigent and Leigh sued Brown's publishers for plagiarism but lost heavily and were left with a three-million-pound legal bill. Baigent sold his home to fund the reparation, but the stress is widely held to have contributed to his death from a brain haemorrhage in 2013 at age sixty-five.

Riddell notes that during their friendship the Holy Blood and Holy Grail theme was already well established in Baigent's mind. They, along with album cover designer Tony Aspland, sought to employ iconography of this theme in the album's cover art (Figure 4.1).[8]

Cover design

Tony Aspland, a Channel Islander from Jersey, was another friend of Riddell's. Working as a graphic designer in Auckland, Aspland's expertise clearly fitted the bill. Aspland was familiar with the band's music and the other musicians as, for a time, he lived with Riddell.

When contacted by this author in 2021, Aspland happily replied, 'Alastair, Peter and the young skinny drummer . . . [and the] practice sessions in the shed at Horopito Street I remember well.'[9] Pressed further regarding the album cover design though, he remarked, 'Can't remember, however, doing the album cover designs. But then they say if you can remember those years you weren't really there!'[10]

The cover's message

The front cover features Riddell standing alone dressed in a sharply modern multicoloured suit with wide lapels and a bright-red tie that matches his red lips. He stands before lush purple curtains, with his left hand resting upon an ornate table/altar, upon which lies a red rose and a crystal. Lit strongly from his left, Riddell's face is divided into two, into light and dark, creating a sense of duality as moody shadow falls upon the right side while the left is effectively overexposed. Strikingly artful, evocative and carefully staged, the image is clearly an archetypal one. Riddell explains, 'I love William Blake, and I know Michael did, and some of the Christian gnostic ideas that he had. If you look at it from a Jungian point of view, it's just symbolic; it's archetypal. I was obsessed with Jung's ideas of the archetypes.'[11]

Riddell further elaborates his intentions:

I'm kind've like a sartorial clown, hence the multi-coloured suit. Always having the flip side to things. People will wonder, 'Why is there a crystal there?' In Buddhism the crystal is a symbol of enlightenment. If we can raise our conscious frequency we can see that all things are related and have a world of peace. The red rose, on the other hand, is symbolic of the blood that we shed.[12]

The low resolution of the image adds atmosphere, removing clinical specificity, sabotaging reality and conveying an almost dream-like state. 'I wanted it grainy', says Riddell, 'although it came out a little more grainy than I wanted'.[13]

The front cover strongly suggests that the album is a solo effort, given that only Riddell is present; the other four relegated to the rear. But it was never intended to be so divisive. The single sleeve that encased the record was originally planned as a gatefold cover. If one turns the cover over, it is clear that the front and rear images are actually a single photograph that wraps around the entirety of the cover. Therefore, it would have been possible to open the cover to display all five musicians within the same frame. Riddell explains, 'If you cut the cover round the seam, you'll notice we are all in the same space.'[14] Changing the design of the cover to a single sleeve also removed the possibility for further artwork and photographs inside, which would have shown Riddell and the other musicians in each other's company instead of distanced. Riddell says, 'There was to have been another shoot for the inside pictures. EMI put the kibosh on the fold-out at the last minute.'[15] Peter Cuddihy, who was living with Riddell at the time, recalls his friend's reaction upon hearing the news of the change: 'Yeah, he was pretty pissed off about that, actually.'[16]

Recording the album

In January 1975 the band set off from Auckland for EMI Studios, Wakefield Street, Wellington. Riddell and Raynor travelled with Eccles in his van along with all of the band's equipment, while Cuddihy and Clark flew down. Cuddihy elaborates: 'Alastair offered to fly Greg and I to Wellington to record the Space Waltz album as I was playing four nights a week in a night club with The Human Instinct and Greg was working full time.'[17] Eccles remembers:

> We put nine of Alastair's songs together and drove to Wellington to the EMI studios in the middle of the city. It was an eight track studio in need of much repair and maintenance. Alan Galbraith was the producer. He had a good empathy with the band and, more importantly, Alastair had a fair amount of confidence in his ability.[18]

Unquestionably, all band members approached the recording with equal enthusiasm and commitment. Greg Clark's recollection is typical of the vibe: 'I was only twenty years old at the time and the whole experience was new and exciting. I had been in covers bands . . . but this was a first playing original music. It was a thrilling and harmonious environment to be in.'[19]

Upon arrival in Wellington the band initially stayed together in a serviced apartment booked for them by EMI. Of their time in the studio, Cuddihy recalls:

> We recorded the main parts of the whole album in three days, which nowadays would be unheard of! Tony [Raynor] stayed

on and did overdubs with Alastair. Alastair then completed the production with Alan. Because we were well rehearsed and had all spent a good period of time practicing in 'the shed' – Alastair's back garden man-cave and composing room – we managed to get an excellent result.[20]

Well rehearsed they were, with the only unknown quantity in terms of musical performance being the contribution, away from the mixing desk, of Galbraith. But he too seemed to grasp what was required to bring Riddell's songs to life. Riddell recalls, 'Alan made suggestions and added things like handclaps and synth . . . nothing that didn't sit well in the mix. It was fine, what he did.'[21]

With the album tracks recorded, Eccles, Cuddihy and Clark left for home, while Riddell and Raynor moved into Galbraith's Eastbourne home for the next stage of the process. Once his overdubs were completed, Raynor too left for Auckland, leaving Riddell in Wellington to undertake mixing with Galbraith. Raynor provides a fond recollection:

I remember staying with Alan Galbraith, who was an affable type (he worked for EMI and we were told he was to be our producer), meeting and going fishing with his neighbour Sam Neill, going to EMI studios, and simply playing the songs just as we'd rehearsed them after the red recording button was pressed and someone said 'Rolling'. I remember there was some talk of 'adjusting the azimuth', which was gobbledegook to me, but which later turned out to be an important factor in the sonic quality (or not) of the record. I thought we did pretty well playing the songs and it all seemed over very quickly, with few keyboard overdubs. (Prior to this, I had no idea what an overdub was). Alastair was more au fait with the recording process. He seemed more au fait with most things, actually. Anyway, knowing nothing about mixing, I wasn't needed for the album mixdown. Alastair stayed on for that and I somehow made my way back to Auckland.[22]

Galbraith's memories of the recording and subsequent mixing are positive ones. He observes, 'The sessions were quite happy I thought. Alastair and Tony stayed at my house in Eastbourne. We got on well and it all seemed quite relaxed at the time.'[23]

Providing something of a caveat to this is Riddell's recollection that time ran out towards the end of the recording and mixing as EMI became unhappy with the amount of time being taken. As a result, Riddell believes, some of the intended overdubs were sacrificed, particularly further backing vocals from the band members (not those of the Yandall Sisters). This view is not shared by Galbraith, and Riddell's bandmates do not recall any tension during their time in Wellington. However, they returned to Auckland before Riddell; Cuddihy does remember that Riddell was unhappy with EMI when he subsequently returned from Wellington, although Cuddihy is unaware of any specific cause.

Production

An album's production is always a subjective and potentially divisive topic, and upon release, *Space Waltz by Alastair Riddell* would prove as contentious as any with contrasting views from critics, a debate that was subsequently and very publicly joined by both artist and producer. These views will be examined in the upcoming section dealing with the album's reception. During this current framing of the recording, however, it is useful to have an insight into the producer's intentions. Galbraith outlines his view:

> As a producer, part of my job is to get to grips with a wide selection of musical styles and ideas. [Riddell] was the artist, I'm there to help him get his ideas on tape. I know that later Alastair became quite critical of the production, but at the time I don't recall him being unhappy.[24]

While *Space Waltz by Alastair Riddell* is often held up in historical appraisals as being New Zealand's pre-eminent (even solitary) glam rock album, Galbraith doesn't recall any specific request from Riddell to achieve a particular stylistic allegiance, glam or otherwise. His personal belief is that the sound

> comes from the songs themselves and the way they are played/arranged. We were obviously limited in the HMV studio as far as the latest equipment was concerned and also in the finer points of production when compared to the UK studios. However, Alastair's musical style was not a million miles away from a lot of other basic UK rock. It was the songs that made it different and his guitar playing that relied heavily on double tracking and harmonising. The name 'glam rock' covers a wide range of styles from bands like Bowie, to Sweet, Mud et al. I think it refers mostly to the image of the band rather than a specific musical style. I just work with what the band gives me and what I think they want to hear. I always tried not to be a copyist but to always look for what set the artist apart.[25]

Space Waltz: A band or a solo venture?

Were Space Waltz a band in the traditional sense, or was it an Alastair Riddell solo project supported by obliging backing musicians/friends who were potentially interchangeable/ replaceable?

When Riddell, Cuddihy, Eccles, Raynor and Clark first came to the attention of the nation on *Studio One/New Faces*, they were unequivocally introduced as a band; 'a fulltime band', in the words of presenter Craig Little. If I might consider myself typical of the viewing public at the time, then my belief was that this was a fully unified band. While Riddell was clearly the focal point, I nevertheless saw them as a single unit, just as Split Ends, with Tim Finn at the forefront, had been the previous year. What I didn't realize was that although Little was correct in stating that the five members were a bona fide working band, that description related to Stewart and the Belmonts, their cover band's alter ego. Space Waltz was an entirely different venture, an experiment. This situation would be borne out when Riddell's signature was the only one to appear on the contract offered by EMI. Galbraith reveals, 'Only Alastair signed the EMI contract. He gave us the impression that the band was just a backing group put together for the occasion and may change going forward.'[26] But, of course, the general public had no inkling of this.

Studio One/New Faces continued to progress towards the final, and Riddell found himself in demand. He alone was the subject of many interviews across various media. In *Hot Licks*, writer Derek King introduced his two-page interview with

Riddell as follows: 'Alastair, fronting a temporary group for that occasion [*Studio One/New Faces*], is at the time of writing one of the leading contenders.'[27] Further into the interview, Riddell clarified the situation:

> It's hard to get good musicians together who don't have some sort of allegiance to a steady band. I've been forced to go out on my own because I can't offer a steady income to the musicians I'd like to work with. You can hold a group together for a while but if you're not involved in regular work you can't expect it to last. I've developed my style independent of a group so I can arrange and produce it on my own and run the whole thing. I know how it must sound so I don't rely on anybody else. . . . Being on my own is probably a good thing when it comes to my serious music because it's given me confidence as a composer.[28]

Nevertheless, the band-or-solo-artist uncertainty continued. EMI's promotional posters for the release of the 'Out on the Street' single featured a candid photograph of Riddell only but accompanied by the words, 'Space Waltz: our new single "Out on the Street" is now available.'

In his 'Sound Round' column in the *New Zealand Listener*, Ray Columbus made the situation clearer ahead of the debut tour, for which Cuddihy was unavailable. Columbus announced:

> The group is mostly a vehicle to display the talents of composer/singer/guitarist and front man Alastair Riddell and, in that respect, it does well. The lineup of the group for its forthcoming tour includes two members of Split Enz who are only with Alastair for the tour and will remain with Split Enz. They are Mike Chunn (bass) and Tony Raynor (keyboards). The

permanent members of Space Waltz are Greg Clark (guitar) and Brent Eccles (drums).[29]

When the album was released, its title, *Space Waltz by Alastair Riddell*, left little doubt that Space Waltz was, in its creator's mind at least, primarily a solo venture. Indeed, the title took Riddell's four musical collaborators by surprise as they had assumed it would be released under the Space Waltz name. Their opinions on the matter vary to this day.

Raynor: 'Eventually, the album was released. Alastair posed alone on the front cover, the band on the back cover . . . the title being *Space Waltz by Alastair Riddell* . . . which I, for one, was a little taken aback by, at the time.'[30]

Eccles describes his reaction as one of 'Total shock and surprise and I didn't know what to do. I just got on with it and was as supportive and loyal to "the band" as I could be.'[31]

Clark: 'I had no problem with it as Alastair wrote and owned the rights to all the songs. His choice at the time and I was not connected.'[32]

Cuddihy: 'I just didn't "go there" with him about it. I didn't want to get caught up in any angst and was quite happy to cruise along for the ride.'[33]

In an interview with the author, Riddell explained his reasoning:

The reason I put my name on it was because Ed was leaving the band. He'd given me the word literally just days after we'd recorded the album. He said, 'I'm out. Split Enz are going to Australia and I'm going with them.' So I thought, 'I'm gonna put my name on that album. It's going to be "Alastair Riddell and Space Waltz", or "Alastair Riddell Presents Space Waltz", or however I'd word it, because it's going to be important to me long-term that my name is on there. Otherwise I'm just going to end up being a singer in some band. I've got to start promoting myself.'[34]

Further recalling his reaction upon hearing of Raynor's decision to leave, Riddell admits, 'It was devastating, because since 1971 it had been our dream. We had a number-one hit and we had an album in the can, ready to be released. And he's gonna leave the band!'[35]

Although it's clear that due to the nature of the EMI contract Riddell could have taken any four musicians into the studio with him, it's equally obvious that the magic of the work is due to the combination of the talents of all five musicians. Riddell, Cuddihy, Eccles, Clark and Raynor knew each other well, had played together a lot and had all shared the tumultuous and very public *Studio One/New Faces* ride. In all respects, except a solitary signature on a contract, they were a band.

Reception

The much-awaited album was released in April 1975. Due to the album's extraordinary and very public back story, reviewers were practically falling over themselves to offer their critique. Despite this enthusiasm many of them engaged in the then-prevalent practice of judging the quality of any local release by firstly drawing comparisons to overseas acts. The local act would almost always come out second best in these match-ups, seen as inferior and often derivative.

This practice was part of a wider debilitating phenomenon termed Cultural Cringe (aka Colonial Cringe) that still had a firm grip on New Zealand arts and culture. While this phenomenon has arguably almost completely evaporated today, other colonial outposts, including Canada and most especially New Zealand's nearest neighbour Australia, experienced the same artistic devaluation and disregard for their own culture during the course of the twentieth century. In essence, Cultural Cringe was the flawed notion that only the arts and culture of far older and more established countries with longer and prouder histories possessed true value. Art and Culture were to be found predominantly in Europe, especially 'Mother England'. A head-shaking example of Cultural Cringe flowing from the fingers of a rock music reviewer is the following excerpt from a 1976 critique of New Zealand band Ragnarok. Contemporaries of Riddell and Space Waltz and Split Enz, Christchurch band Ragnarok are today revered as pioneers of New Zealand progressive rock. Yet, at the time, critic David MacLennan opined haughtily that they were 'in the vein of Pink Floyd or some of the German bands, highly derivative, and for this reason I doubt they would get far overseas where they have the real thing'.[36] Ouch. Such was the Cultural Cringe-laced environment that local rock bands faced when daring to introduce their artistic wares to the marketplace.

And so, back to 1975 and the launch of *Space Waltz by Alastair Riddell*. In the *Sunday Times*, under the pseudonym Double Track, the reviewer wrote:

It is the first mainstream New Zealand pop-rock album I've heard which I think would survive a review in an overseas rock magazine . . . perhaps the greatest strength of this album is the depth . . . you will not find one weak track here . . . I love this album. I don't mind all the posturing and all the words. I think beneath it all Riddell is both a talented fellow, and a very talented songwriter.[37]

Under the title 'A Riddle: A True Star?', *Hot Licks* afforded the album two separate and very contrasting reviews. One of these reviewers, Brian Thurgood, was effusive in his praise:

Alastair appears as a major song-writing talent (he's been respected by musicians for years) and this album is definitely world class, in fact it's better than most overseas albums I've heard lately. . . . This album warrants a close listen by all those who work in music or records, who treat listening to music as a rewarding activity, and who like to keep up with significant, outstanding music. If you really get off on good music without all the intellectual crap, this will suit you too.[38]

The second *Hot Licks* reviewer, Blanx, took a rather different view:

Alastair has a problem and this is the downfall of Space Waltz. He has the thesis off pat (off David actually) but he rarely introduces an antithesis (another influence or even some of his own musical personality where'er it lurk) and I think he only ever really makes the all important synthesis twice. So you're left with Influences without Direction.[39]

In *The Star*, Rob White's view fell somewhere in between:

Alistair [*sic*] Riddell candidly admits he is not altogether pleased with the debut Space Waltz album because it was rushed. On hearing it, I agree with him. Alistair said he had very little time to sit down and write material and less than three weeks to teach the band the songs. The group has done a good job, particularly the synthesiser work of Raynor. The weight of the album lies in the first side which is taken up mainly with material we have heard already – the two singles 'Out in the Street' and 'Fraulein Love', and the other New Faces song, 'Beautiful Boy'. Best of the bunch however is 'Seabird', which Alistair wrote while he was in Auckland's Orbe [*sic*], before his television success. Alistair's faults (and I think that these are mainly due to the speed the record had to be taped) show on the second side. All nine songs on the LP were written by Alistair and he had the same trouble as his favourite band Genisis [*sic*] – he is too wordy. If it was not for some clever hook lines the songs could easily drag. These lines indicate he is capable of short, punchy songs that still include many of his dramatic lyrics . . . his debut LP shows that although weak in places, Alistair Riddell is well on the way to becoming an artist equal to those overseas if he can produce songs like 'Seabird' and 'Open Up'.[40]

And what was the view of David MacLennan, the sharp-penned nemesis of Ragnarok? 'Outside of Australasia Riddell hasn't got a dog's show. The music is far too derivative of the Bowie/Roxy school of high camp that went out of fashion in '73. In England or America, darling Alastair would be howled off the stage.'[41]

In a separate review written for *Salient*, Victoria University's student newspaper, the same author offered a fuller critique. MacLennan wrote:

Most music writers have completely missed the point as far as Alastair Riddell is concerned. He's a smart cookie: he wants to make good music, something which New Zealand has produced very little of up to now. However, he realises that a local artist cannot lay a 'head'-music trip (for want of a better term) on the public, and be musically and commercially accepted; sadly, the New Zealand public has little faith in the abilities of local musicians. Therefore, he figures, he has to put himself in a strong position commercially – become popular and sell lotsa records. He looks around at the music scene and asks: 'What is selling at the moment?' The answer? – Bowie and lesser imitators . . . and as such is strongly influenced by the Bowie/Roxy school of vocalese and instrumentalism. Riddell's biggest handicap is that he sounds like Bowie and Ferry rolled into one.[42]

I (the author) vividly recall at age fifteen buying *Space Waltz by Alastair Riddell* from the local record store and cycling home with it in great excitement. Once safely home, I placed it with great care upon the turntable of my bedroom stereo and cranked it up. Unlike the album's official reviewers discussed earlier, I had no inclination or predisposition to hold the image-laden aural world that unfolded around me up against anything else from anywhere else. This was Alastair Riddell and Space Waltz, from New Zealand. End of story.

But then I was only in my early teens and far less invested in, or even aware of, the kind of cultural quagmire that a presumably older reviewer such as Blanx seemingly wallowed in. He continued:

When I professed a slight distaste for this disc, friends leapt to its defence with a rousing 'But it's GOOD for New Zealand'. An open invitation to the traditional complacency which riddles this society on every level. But also a statement which presupposes an indigenous music culture which just doesn't exist. . . . So this album will have a lot of attention focused on it for reasons other than its intrinsic merit. Space Waltz highlights the problems of a progressive artist in the land of the long white Culchur Gulch.[43]

In the following issue of *Hot Licks*, producer Alan Galbraith responded directly to Blanx:

I really feel sorry for reviewers and critics (normally this country only produces the latter) who are asked to review local artists' efforts, after all, the poor guy has no previous reviews to swat up, no rave publicity articles to precede his listening, no overseas ratings, no built in safety factor at all. He just has to lay his knowledge and reputation right on the line. That must be tough when you're not a trained recording engineer or an experienced producer or successful artist – real tough. However any review should be taken as one person's point of view so I guess it's not that important. To Mr Blanx I say – compare Riddell to Bowie? What about Bowie to Brel, Poco to Little Feat, Bay City Rollers to The Glitter Band, Sparks to Split Enz (I heard Split Enz first) and so on and so on. You should know better than to believe that anything in popular music is entirely original. I have heard that you have been a good friend of Alistair's for some time – perhaps that's how you became so aware of his influences and maybe just a little jealousy (local boy makes good) prompts you to remind us all of the fact that our boy is not entirely original either. Has no one seen the similarities between Riddell and Ray Davies or even Jagger, does it even matter?

I am led to believe through this review that you have a slight distaste for the local scene in general, which is rather sad when you really think about it, because believe me, it is going to develop far beyond your expectations. Personally, I chuckle at any mention of intellectualism regarding Alastair Riddell's work when I watch him 'colour' his melodies with words that 'sound' and 'feel' good – the mark of a true artist – and what's more, a 'Popstar' (and not ashamed of it).[44]

Offering my own view again, at age fifteen I just wanted a great album from a band that had impacted significantly upon my world. And I got it. In my view, there was no 'Culchur Gulch'. For Blanx, it seemed that the album proved such a thing existed. To me, the album proved that it didn't. The 'problems of a progressive artist' in New Zealand had not been highlighted. If anything, they had been solved.

Recalling his reaction to buying the album at age thirteen, Don McGlashan too cared not for any lofty and superfluous question of influence. He remarks, 'I took it home to my bedroom and puzzled and shivered over the lyrics. I wanted to fill in the gaps – dreaming up powders, phials, needles and strange sex in seedy city apartments. My thirteen-year-old imagination lunged at the songs like a Bobby calf at the feed bucket.'[45]

In a joint complaint to the editor of *Hot Licks*, three readers voiced similar frustration: 'Some of us are a bit fed up at the way your magazine seems to judge local talent by how closely they imitate overseas artists, e.g. Space Waltz – Roxy Music and John Hanlon – Cat Stevens . . . How much longer will people ignore genuinely unique artists?'[46]

The wildly contrasting views regarding the album were not confined to the musical content alone. The production too came in for considerable debate. To this day I hear nothing wrong with the production; it's an intrinsic part of the equation that made the album what it was, and is, to me. With a notable emphasis on high and low frequencies, arguably at the expense of mids, perhaps, certain features, such as Eccles' cymbals, gain emphasis – more so than on other releases. Meanwhile, the spatial effects on the vocals reinforce an otherworldliness that is, to this listener, entirely in keeping with the subject matter. But Riddell himself was dissatisfied, something he confided to Roger Jarrett, editor of *Hot Licks*, who wrote, 'Alastair has serious reservations about the album, ("it's like a dark blot in my memory compared to what I know I could do") and while insisting no one was solely responsible, felt it could've been far superior as the songs were good songs but suffered through lack of rehearsal time and many extraneous factors.' He added, with more specificity regarding the album's production, that it was 'so noisy . . . too much reverb'.[47]

Blanx is another who found fault with the production, describing it as a 'muddy mix and almost indecipherable bass . . . suffering from the blandness which renders NZMOR music (Rumour, Hanlon) a load of wimp'.[48] This view was immediately countered on the same page by co-reviewer Brian Thurgood, who praised Galbraith's work, stating, 'The production, often a stumbling block with NZ albums, is better than many overseas albums.'[49]

In his review in *Salient*, David MacLennan put the boot in. He surprisingly took on one of the world's heavyweights to make his point:

My biggest complaint about this one is the recording quality: some of the most unimaginative engineering I've heard since the Beatles. The drums stay in one place, the keyboards stay in one place – whassamatter with EMI? After all, 'Atom Heart Mother' was done, like this one, on an eight-track machine. EMI should send their engineers overseas to learn how to do the job right.[50]

Showing surprising restraint, producer Alan Galbraith responded to the criticism in his letter to *Hot Licks*. He wrote:

Unlike Alastair I'm not about to apologise or make any excuses about local facilities. After all I have had numerous hit records out of the studio that album was recorded in. There are production faults on the album many of them purely my fault – not the engineer, not the eight track facilities, not the 12 inch Goodmans that are used for monitoring, not the record company telling me to 'finish it in three days', no way. Alastair and I goofed a little here and there that's all. It was his first real recording session ever and it was my introduction to his music. The nearest thing to it that I had ever been involved in was the music of Jacques Brel.[51]

Just as the band's performance on *Studio One/New Faces* polarized viewers, *Space Waltz by Alastair Riddell* divided listeners. The album raised questions of artistic merit, certainly, as one would expect in the reviewing of any kind of artistic endeavour, but it also graphically brought to the surface myriad attitudes and prejudices derived from Cultural Cringe. *Space Waltz by Alastair Riddell* problematized what it was to create a New Zealand album, not just the compositional and performative aspects but also the technical side of music production.

Sales

Unfortunately, the officially compiled and recognized New Zealand Album Chart wasn't established until the last week of April 1975, at least two weeks after *Space Waltz by Alastair Riddell* was released. The album appeared on the newly launched chart in the first three weeks of its existence, reaching #14 on 25 April, #15 on 2 May and #31 on 9 May, before dropping off. Thus, there is no sure way of knowing how it performed in those first couple of weeks of its release.

While individual band members today recall mention of it possibly having reached gold record status (5,000 units at the time), this seems unlikely. As EMI staff from the era advised, the initial pressing was almost certainly the standard (for the day) five hundred units, and no second pressing was undertaken. For comparison's sake, two other notable releases that year were debut albums from Split Enz (*Mental Notes*) and Ragnarok (their self-titled album). Neither of these releases went anywhere near gold status either, in an era in which albums by New Zealand acts struggled greatly in their home country.

Official sales figures for the album are no longer available. When EMI (NZ) was taken over by Universal Music NZ in 2013, the accompanying documentation did not include historical sales figures from the 1970s. As the current chairman of Universal Music NZ, Adam Holt, notes, 'EMI (like many companies) changed their systems over the years and cumulative sales weren't necessarily carried over to new systems.'[52]

Complicating the issue is the fact that copies of the Space Waltz album were also released under the HMV and WRC (World Record Club) labels in addition to the primary EMI release. However, even in the extremely unlikely event that these print runs had matched EMI's run of five hundred units, this would still have left the album well short of the threshold for gold record status.

5 The album part 2

Central theme

'We're half cut on moonbeams' ('Scars of Love' side 2 track 3)

> I spent the first years of the 1970s in a microcosm; a self-imposed isolation from the mainstream of popular music and culture. I was engrossed in my own visions: my own mixtures of science fiction, esoteric literature; and my own musical obsessions, a mélange of what was then fairly obscure stuff – the music of Peter Hammill (Van der Graaf Generator), Tom Rapp's Pearls Before Swine, David Bowie, Soft Machine, King Crimson, Kraftwerk, Tangerine Dream, and many others.[1]

The overriding theme of *Space Waltz by Alastair Riddell* is science fiction. Riddell admits to a fascination with the genre and was writing stories at the time. He recalls, 'I was reading science fiction and I was trying to write it. Most of the Space Waltz songs are based on stories and ideas I was tossing around. . . . I had an imaginary planet called Telluria . . . and I was really interested in a kind of mixture of [an] androgynous clone-based future on this planet.'[2]

Science fiction was particularly topical in the early to mid-1970s, especially for artists like Riddell, who'd grown up during the space-crazy 1960s. The 'Space Race' – a hotly contested theatre of the Cold War between the United States and USSR – had only recently culminated, on 20 July 1969, in the Apollo 11 moon landing that saw American astronauts Neil Armstrong and Edwin (Buzz) Aldrin walk on the moon. Literature and arts of all disciplines were saturated with science fiction throughout the decade. As President John F. Kennedy predicted in his 1961 speech before a joint session of the US Congress, 'I believe that this nation should commit itself to achieving the goal, before this decade is out, of landing a man on the moon and returning home safely to earth. No single space project . . . will be more exciting, or more impressive to mankind.'[3] Meanwhile Robert Jones, an authority on the manifestation of science fiction in popular culture and the arts, suggested, 'By the mid-1960s the exploration of space had become a fact of everyday life for everybody in the world, and many people with no previous interest followed it avidly.'[4]

At the same time, the threat of nuclear war was ever-present. Humankind's love affair with technology might well spell doom for our planet. The justifiable fear of the 'big red button', with its attendant threat of mutual annihilation, particularly occupied the thoughts of the younger generations who'd grown up with military chest-beating and nuclear stockpiling. There was also the nightmare of the Vietnam War. The idealism and promise of the 1960s counterculture had faded, and while rock music retained its position as the flagbearer of youth culture, some of its greatest heroes had succumbed. Jimi Hendrix, Jim Morrison, Janis Joplin and Brian Jones were all dead, and the Beatles had split acrimoniously. As the 1960s surrendered to the 1970s, love, it seemed, was no longer all you needed.

No wonder writers and artists the world overlooked to solutions in the stars. If life on Earth was so tenuous, what might science offer humankind? Life on other planets? Contact with aliens? Cloning? Artists in all mediums explored other worlds, alien landscapes, hybrid life forms and pondered how the very essence of what it is to be human might change. What might human love become? How would sex and reproduction work? Would mind control wipe out freedom of thought and human emotion? How far could AI (artificial intelligence) go? Could human hybrids be pre-programmed to think and act in certain ways? Might HAL9000 – Stanley Kubrick's murderous computer in *2001: A Space Odyssey* – become a reality? Such pondering offered much fodder to creative-thinking musicians, sometimes with the aid of mind-altering drugs and sometimes not.

The well-read Riddell found plenty of artistic stimulation in his considerable knowledge of history, philosophy, politics, art and literature. He observed:

> With 'Out on the Street', and eventually with most of the Space Waltz album material, I essentially drew a metaphor between the much-claimed 'dawning of the age of Aquarius' and the mounting horrors of world politics, pollution, the Bomb, and selfishness in general that were slowly dawning on our collective consciousness. We had recently witnessed the horrors of the war in Vietnam, and New Zealand had sent frigates to protest the French Nuclear program at Mururoa.[5]

Thematically, then, the Space Waltz album pivots on juxtapositions, on explorations of duality, of dichotomies between good and evil, human and technological, even, in Riddell's words, 'a kind of Queen/whore thing . . . a sign of Aphrodite or a grave apocalypse'.[6]

From this deep well came Riddell's Telluria. Its genetically engineered inhabitants, the Tellurians – a race which uses sex purely as a reproductive process involving no emotional love – are introduced in the very first song on the album, 'Fräulein Love'.

The songs

The latter half of 1974 and early 1975 passed by in a rush for Space Waltz as *Studio One/New Faces* changed everything. A nation was watching and waiting, and so was a record company. One hit single did not make a career despite the instant star status bestowed upon them by the nation's youth and media. A contract was signed, and an album's worth of material needed to be delivered quickly in order to meet everyone's expectations. By the end of their television journey, Riddell had just three songs, four at a pinch, fully written and rehearsed with his band. While the concept for the album was clear in his mind, he had less than half an album's worth of material ready to go. However, he had bare bones for the rest of the tracks:

> I already had embryos for all of them. Most of them had titles and bits of choruses and I could present them to the band on either piano or guitar, but the biggest thing I didn't have was all the lyrics. So the panic was when I had to finish the lyrics. There was a lot of work to do to get them to what I would call 'studio ready'.[7]

Intense work began, for Riddell especially, but also for the rest of the band once their leader had presented his bare new works to them. With everyone excited and committed, rehearsal in Riddell's back shed began in earnest. While Riddell lamented in interviews after the album's release that he did not have longer for this process, the musicians clearly used their time well and delivered remarkably in the studio.

'Fräulein Love'

Oh well the summer is breaking and the Fräuleins are singing
Iced drinks on a Saturday night
With Martinis on the rocks
They'll try to sting you, try to bring you down
The caviar's fine and Margery's looking divine
Oh won't you please slow down – I get confused at this pace
Oh won't you please slow down – Your behaviour's so
    misleading
You and me conversing here – Oh we're not in any race

Chorus:
Fräulein Love matters nothing to me
And the waiter, ice only please, I hope you don't find
    everything's
Fräulein Love matters nothing to me
I would love to deny those lies, that I in truth don't despise
Fräulein Love is a corporeal truth
But you can rise above it if you try

I can't say it much stronger – Please don't take any longer
Than you have to do – I'm enamoured of you
It's not the senses I play for
Not the Fräulein like Raynor

But a life more complete – and not just bonbons to eat
Oh won't you please slow down – I get confused at this pace
Oh won't you please slow down – Your behaviour's so
    misleading
You and me conversing here – Oh we're not in any race

Repeat chorus
Two of a kind – Oh out of our minds
But if we concentrate we will surely find love
I get a feeling there's a bond so strange
I get a feeling quite complete inside
I feel blessed only when you're near me
I guess it's really love
I guess it's really something more than Tellurian love

Repeat chorus ×2

'Fräulein Love' provides an emphatic opening, and it's no surprise the song was chosen for the second single.

Riddell's introductory guitar riff builds in intensity during its three repetitions as the other musicians join in one by one, creating a swell that pulls the song – and the listener – inexorably forward into the action. The chord sequence is a I-II-IV progression (C-D-F) played over a C pedal with the major supertonic (II) appearing instead of the far more common minor supertonic, therefore ensuring a powerful harmonic statement (Lydian) in these earliest moments of the album. An Eccles snare fill announces the entry of the beat proper, and from that moment, things take off. One particular point of note – a clever touch – is that in the verses the I-II-IV progression of the introduction undergoes an exact inversion, becoming a I-VII-V (C-Bb-G). While in essence a fairly straightforward rocker of a song with no rhythmic deviation from its 4/4 heart, clever dynamic shifts ensure listener interest is maintained throughout. Simply, 'Fräulein Love' stays powerful and exciting for its full duration. The vibe is frenetic, even manic, but Riddell pulls a trick at the point where he sings 'Oh won't you *please slow down*', switching to crotchets for the last three words in place of the incessant quavers, thereby effectively word-painting. The bridge that separates the final two choruses also skilfully changes the pace while not diminishing the intensity and serves to bring the underlying sentiment up close and personal: 'I guess it's *really* love!'

Love is a universal theme in popular songwriting. But this is not your average love song; no standard girls-in-summer effort. In fact, despite its Kiwi origins, the subjects of affection are 'Fräuleins'. This term is foreign to antipodean ears. Alien, even. It's the same tactic that David Bowie employed when describing Ziggy Stardust as 'like some cat from Japan', then going on to visually underline the alien(ation) trope he'd created by treading the stage clad in Kansai Yamamoto's superb Japanese costumes.

Riddell's use of 'Tellurian' is a masterstroke as, in 1975, it sounded both familiar and alien to a young audience comprising the first generation ever raised on television. Many fans just a few years earlier had thrilled to the alien threat posed by the similar-sounding Silurians of *Doctor Who* fame, who'd threatened humankind in the 1970 and 1972 incarnations of the hugely popular BBC programme. Silurian/Tellurian. Whether intentional or not, an alien allusion thus existed for many listeners. This seldom-used word, which must have sent many a fan to a dictionary, ironically denotes an inhabitant of Earth. But in Riddell's hands we are taken well beyond Earth as the love he's experiencing is 'something *more* than Tellurian love'. 'Fräulein Love', then, has ensured that the album is framed by science fiction right from the start.

Riddell's imaginary world, populated by genetically engineered, androgynous clones with sex-less reproduction and a supposed dearth of emotional love, is problematized with the admission between the protagonists of 'a bond so strange'. In this acknowledgement of a mysterious linkage beyond the norm for an android life form (could it be love?), Riddell's knowledge and use of an extensive pool of language and terminology is a feature. 'Corporeal truth', the subject of many a scientific study, is not a term one might expect in a rock song of the day. Historically, it refers to an awareness of and attraction to the physical body – the notion that unadulterated truth lies in body language. In the context of 'Fräulein Love', if clones can, in effect, desire each other, can they really be so inhuman? Perhaps human emotional traces survived the genetic engineering process?

Upon its release as a single, 'Fräulein Love' garnered qualified praise in the Singles column of *Hot Licks* magazine. Reviewer J. M. Cummings opined:

> My favourite New Zealand single artist at the moment is Alastair Riddell, whose 'Fräulein Love' (EMI) is a worthy successor to one of the best singles of last year, 'Out on the Street'. That insufferable Bowie affectation still tinges his vocals, but in the background the Yandell [*sic*] Sisters 'ooh-ooh' effectively and Alastair's guitar work can't be beat.[8]

Yet, charged with following a number-one hit, 'Fräulein Love' ostensibly failed, reaching only number twenty and remaining on the chart for just two weeks. Riddell lamented:

> At the time the second single, 'Fräulein Love', came out, we'd had huge success with 'Out On The Street' and I don't know what people were expecting but it didn't really fit the bill. . . . Of course it was a frustration. I think perhaps we were being too esoteric. I think stylistically it was just a little bit too avant garde, if I can say that, for New Zealand. It wasn't chart oriented in a New Zealand way.[9]

While not disputing Riddell's view, another critical factor is that 'Fräulein Love' did not get the prime-time television exposure that its predecessor so crucially did. The free advertising afforded by the *Studio One/New Faces* promotional clips were pure gold in maintaining the profile of 'Out on the Street'. 'Fräulein Love' was afforded no such thing.

It's also true that 'Fräulein Love' lacked a crucial x-factor highly prominent in 'Out on the Street' – the glam rock-esque super-chorus with its call and response demanding that one join in and sing along.

For those keen on discerning influences, Riddell ensured an easy task with 'Fräulein Love'. Next to the song's title on the handwritten lyric insert, Riddell provided a small dedication: 'Here I say "ta" to Bryan.' He later explained:

> It's a little dedication to Bryan Ferry. You can hear it in my voice. The whole song was supposed to be a bit Ferry-esque. In my head it was some kind of futuristic casino in some distant part of the galaxy. I'm sitting around with Eddie Raynor eating *vol au vents* and drinking dry Martinis. It was kind've tongue in cheek.[10]

Beautiful Boy

Started out a popstar with long hair bleeding on the stage
Thought he had it made
Were there astral voices singing?
Then a stranger said he knew – 'Did I fake it too?'
Or did he really manage somehow to get it on?
Crowned with doubt – steeped in fears
Of misappropriation of another's cheers
Then a voice said 'Someone has to give
And there's love in your heart
My boy you could go far'

Chorus:
He said You Beautiful Boy
We'll wait for you – Won't let you down
He'd die for your beautiful heart – heaven bound
Your Beautiful Boy is singing
Singing in the hearts of children
The wonderful joy of going on
You Beautiful Boy – He'd die for you
Won't let you down
He'd die for your beautiful heart – heaven bound

A pantheon quite mad – I'm frightened
Where do children turn – are we lost?
If they gain this kind of reason
But in myriad forms and almost infinite guises
And faith in this part displays ironically
Subtle disguises – At that I laughed
But the look on his face said all
There were no more questions

They want you to be
It's up to you – No-one's underground

Repeat chorus
Oh yeah, heaven bound
The Beautiful Boy accepted the challenge for what it was
    worth
Of playing a truly difficult line
He thought hard on what had been said. Was it worth the
    obligation? Yes! He smiled
Oh to be posted on walls
Yeah, your Beautiful Boy loves to love
Oh yeah, your Beautiful Boy's smiling now
The wonderful joy, of going on
Yeah, your Beautiful Boy goes on for the rights of the ones who
    know, but never show
They know the ways of those who think they fool with airs
Oh yeah, oh yeah
Your Beautiful Boy's smiling now
The wonderful joy, of going on
Yeah, your Beautiful Boy goes on through the rain and fog with
    a mystic kind of grace
Oh yeah, oh yeah
Your Beautiful Boy's smiling now
The wonderful joy, of going on, and on, and on

Regarded by several critics as a homage to David Bowie, 'Beautiful Boy' was chosen for the final of *Studio One/New Faces*. A sped-up version (compared to the album) was recorded in the NZBC studio, to which the band mimed somewhat awkwardly. The performance can be readily found on YouTube. It's no wonder that Riddell struggled to mime to what he'd recorded just hours earlier. The timing of the free-form lines that make up the lengthy outro defy replication, such is their complexity, and the song did not fit the bill to the extent that others, including 'Fräulein Love' and either 'Scars of Love' or 'Angel', might have done. Both the beginning and end of the song find Riddell employing a vocal technique called *Sprechstimme*, which is a kind of speech-married-to-sung-melody. It's also evident at the beginning and end of 'Out on the Street' but to a shorter, easier extent. In this vocal technique words are not pitched fixedly like they are in a usual melody, and timing is considerably freer, making exact replication difficult.

Too complex to have been effectively recorded so quickly, 'Beautiful Boy' is given the justice it deserves on the album. It is slower in pace and extra sonic space allows a far better groove; the Yandall Sisters in particular shine. With their polished harmonies high and front in the mix, they lend a soulful, even gospel-like quality to the previously troublesome and here significantly extended outro. Riddell's vocals weave in and out, surrendering centre stage to Pauline, Adele and Mary.

Riddell explains the song's subject matter. He remarks:

> [It was] the idea of the popular synthesised icon and/or god. . . . The idea was in the future this icon would be sexually androgynous; ambiguous as well. Would this bright new future be as idyllic in its controlled and manufactured essence as we might expect or rather did it hold a disturbing and destructive element in its very conception?[11]

The soaring of the backing vocals is angelic, lending credence to the song's quasi-religious theme and illustrating the line, 'Were there astral voices singing?'

The line ending in 'get it on' is surely a knowing wink to Marc Bolan and T. Rex, but there is little glam rock in 'Beautiful Boy'. Gone is the chordal simplicity of 'Fräulein Love' and the four-on-the-floor rhythm section. I played this track to Associate Professor Robert Burns, a specialist in progressive rock who has written foundational texts, including *Experiencing Progressive Rock: A Listener's Companion* (Rowman & Littlefield, 2018). Emigrating to New Zealand decades after the Space Waltz story, he came to the song 'cold', so to speak. His verdict? 'That, to me, is a highly polished, well arranged, prog song. The complexity of the drum and bass parts alone is evidence of that even before taking into account the sophisticated harmony with unexpected chords and melody notes.'[12]

Burns's view mirrors mine. It's almost as if, for *Studio One/ New Faces*, Riddell took one of his most complex songs – and a lengthy one at almost five minutes on the album – and attempted to repackage it as a pop song to be squeezed into their allocated three minutes. On the album, however, 'Beautiful Boy' shines.

Seabird

We left you behind a long long time ago
We were all very young – All our futures pristine bright
We left you behind – Illogic ideals cowered in fright
Where the hope of men lay drying on the walls of our paradigm
    flight
Our commitment was firm then – So firm then to our confident
    brave facade
There was no agnostic wind to blow dust from our sheltered
    oh so pious gaze

We were faultless – Faultless in certainty – But so deficient in truth
A race merely crawling – a race of allegorical youth

Chorus:
And we were flying, the silent Seabird reflecting in your eye
Oh she could take you by control – She could let you know
And we were flying, silent Seabird reflecting in your eye
Oh she could take you by control – She could let you come too

We sailed a ship of penultimate dreams – Our wings were
    made of finer things
We railed against the profane thoughts of those who chose to
    doubt our course
A journey of bright hearts in the midst of failing hope
Plagued by ghosts of enemies too frail to inflict too grievous
    a wound
Impervious to their terminal schemes, we found at last our
    strength unseen

Repeat chorus
And you didn't have to learn those reasons – It was all in your heart
And you didn't have to learn – Then we awakened
Because you left the seeds of reason – It was all in your heart
No more that vicious tongue

And now they're lost – They believed that out-redeemed time
But the lie has been found out – It only passes it
And though they want spirits to enforce us and art to enchant
    them
Their ending is despair unless they're saved – Unless they're
    relieved by prayer

Repeat chorus

'Seabird' is the sole survivor from Orb; by all accounts, the most popular song of that earlier band's highly progressive repertoire. Riddell explains:

> It's about the fact that we repeat mistakes from the past without learning the lessons from them, and then we take them into the future. So it's steeped in the overall ideas of the album. That said, I did change the lyrics. The chorus was kind've the same, but not the verses. I maybe filled up the lines a bit too much. Graham Reid said it sounded like I'd swallowed a thesaurus.[13]

The longest track on the album at eight minutes and forty seconds, 'Seabird' was nevertheless severely truncated. As Riddell recalls, 'In Orb, we'd do ten minute improvisations. And in "Seabird" we had a preamble that was probably eight minutes long; that was before the song proper even started!'[14]

For fans who come to Space Waltz via the sublime pop credentials of 'Out on the Street' – which was practically everyone in New Zealand – 'Seabird' must have come as a shock when they first played the album. Cast in the decidedly un-pop-like minor mode of C Dorian – the domain of traditional English folk songs such as 'Greensleeves' and 'Scarborough Fair' – 'Seabird' is an epic journey as much as a song. *Rip It Up* reviewer Francis Stark called it 'a pocket-sized rock opus'.[15] Some reviewers regarded it as the album's highlight, with highly critical *Hot Licks* reviewer Blanx declaring:

> An Orb original, possibly better there because it was more of a direct statement, it had all the conviction which so much of this album seems to lack. Now it's a Concept Piece, a lot

'weightier' but with a real dramatic value which comes closer to realising Alastair's ideal of the theatrical aspect of playing music than anything else here. This track has had a lot of time to develop and its strength derives from that. It isn't a rushed Bowie brushjob, it's a Riddell track more than anything else. Hurray the Brightest Hope.[16]

'Seabird' is no quick thrill. There is none of the frenetic pace and vibe of 'Fräulein Love' or the other rockers. Rather, it unfolds like a mist around your legs, sinuous, sensuous even, unhurried. It is a brave track, and, if one looks for a descriptor, glam rock does not fit the bill.

This song demonstrates the prowess of the musicians as a unit. Eccles brings the track in alone, his drums exposed in a sparse bass/snare/bass/bass/flam pattern, until joined by Raynor's A.R.P.-derived flute sounds that provide an eerie accompaniment. Once joined by Cuddihy on bass, the solidity and feel of the rhythm section throughout the song is something to relish, providing a rock-solid platform for the two guitarists and the piano of Raynor, who excels on the track with his virtuosity and sensitivity. Which is not to say that the drum and bass parts remain simple. Just the opposite in fact; they are often highly complex. Crucially, Riddell's vocals are placed right at the forefront of the mix, every syllable as clear as a bell for the listener, evocative and highly nuanced. His double-tracked guitar soloing, also up front and close in the mix, provides ample evidence of his axe talents, pulling off soaring passages in keeping with the song's title. It is the space between the notes though that makes this track a winner. Even in the full-on passages, of which there are many, the song breathes unhurriedly. The A.R.P. ripples away in the background throughout, tasteful, unobtrusive and just rightly there as 'Seabird' kills the very concept of time.

It is on 'Seabird' that Riddell makes his strongest case for uniqueness, proving he is not some kind of copycat as some have suggested. Graham Reid might have playfully accused him of swallowing a thesaurus, but the beauty of Riddell's words is evident. Who among the artists that Riddell is held to have emulated would have written 'Where the hope of men lay drying on the walls of our paradigm flight', or 'There was no agnostic wind to blow dust from our sheltered oh so pious gaze'? As Alan Galbraith suggested, Riddell had the talent and confidence to choose words based upon the sound they made when sung. Certain words have a musicality all of their own, and Riddell not only finds them but weaves them into passages and concepts that make wider conceptual sense. It's a very long way from basic meat & veg rock'n'roll. As friend and lifelong musical collaborator Peter Cuddihy notes of Riddell's language prowess, 'It's one of the things that I most admire about him'.[17]

A final word on 'Seabird' from Associate Professor Robert Burns: 'That track is as prog as it gets.'[18]

Out on the Street

Watch out young love
Yeah it's a loser's game
Oh, but you know that now

Who's the lady who whispers lightning from her lips
Some sign of Aphrodite or a grave apocalypse

Don't ask this child for guidance don't ask for strength or glory
Don't follow her directives till you've heard her tell her story
And when she dances she spins pirouettes in fire
You can't maintain defences while the lady plays desire
Gone with all our chances, all the gazes and the glances
Of a boy who tried to follow her to what does she aspire?

Chorus:
She's out on the street – and she talks to everyone she meets
She's no illusion – She tells me she's right but she knows that
    she's wrong

With prayers of hope I tried to reconcile my fears
The chances of survival as she crucifies the years
She says living's a hoax, that no one has the answers
So she spits at love, jibes my tears, mocks time as she dances

Repeat chorus
Oh yes she'll vamp around town trying so hard to be cool
And wanton and she moves with the sound – God the lady
    never frowns
Though she's pushing me away – That's alright, she's okay

Repeat chorus
She knows she's wrong
But it's hard to be brave when all the breaks are against you
Yeah it's hard to be brave when all the breaks are against you

Riddell has described being out on the street in 1970s
Auckland. He recalls:

In 1970 I had a friend who had a flat at the top end of Queen
Street. He had a big stereo and no neighbours to complain

about the noise. He also had a good friend who owned the best record shop in town, and who was a constant source of anything new and strange in the world of contemporary music. This was where we frequently ended up of an evening in 1970 and most of 1971, and it was where we shared our passion of listening to what we regarded as avant-garde and rock and popular music. Many evenings were spent listening in rapture and in altered states to the wonderful and (at the time) little known artists we adored … evenings of magical music, late-night cheese toasties, and thick shakes from the West Wind Dairy. The West Wind was a few doors down from my friend's place, and the only open-all-night dairy in Auckland at the time. We would spend hours listening to, and musically dissecting, our various musical selections, and then at two or three in the morning we would wander down Queen Street, past the transvestites waiting in the doorways for their custom, and sometimes exchange words with the occasional lonely cop on the beat.[19]

It's a safe bet that everyone reading this book will be familiar with 'Out on the Street'. It remains an iconic song, regarded as New Zealand's glam rock anthem. Music writer Simon Sweetman stated:

> To me this is a great Kiwi song because it's reflecting a Kiwi point of view; there's an observation there. This is similar in a way to some of McGlashan's songs, like 'Dominion Road', and even to Hello Sailor's 'Ponsonby Reggae'. There's observations of what's going on in the street around him.[20]

At a perfect-for-radio three minutes and twenty seconds, 'Out on the Street' is the shortest song on the album. Its pop credentials are immense and of their time. The chorus especially is pure glam rock with its compound quadruple (12/8) shuffle feel effortlessly aligning it to 'Can the Can' by Suzi Quatro, 'Jean Genie' by David Bowie, 'Hot Love' and 'Metal Guru' by T. Rex, 'School's Out' by Alice Cooper and numerous others. What is unusual, however, is that the meter changes several times, with the verses being in 4/4. In addition, rhythmic truncation occurs: a half bar of 6/8 at the end of the chorus ('she knows that she's wrong') and another of 2/4 in the bridge section ('the lady never frowns').

The melody is mainly diatonic and pop-friendly with occasional fleeting moments of chromaticism but nothing to undermine the singalong quality, particularly of the all-important chorus. And this song is all about the chorus. A powerful perfect cadence with parallel octaves in both melody and instruments draws the listener forward, while other glam/pop signifiers abound, especially the ever-present antiphony (call and response) that occurs between lead and backing vocals. The chorus is infectious and easy. Replication in the schoolyard, the street or the factory, a cinch for even the most unsophisticated musical ear.

> She's out (OUT) on the street (OUT ON THE STREET)
> And she talks to everyone she meets (OUT ON THE STREET)

The title contains a subtle double entendre, with the subject being literally out on the street or 'out' on the street, in a gender sense. Riddell notes, 'There they were, out on the street and they were stunning. There was no value judgement, they were simply gorgeous people and we would say hi and chat to them.'[21]

While it's safe to assume that few listeners/viewers grasped the deeper meaning behind the lyrics when the song first came to public consciousness, when considered in the context of the album, it clearly fits with Riddell's wider raison d'être and embracing of duality. He explicates:

> The song is quite intellectual and I really don't think a lot of people picked up on the science-fiction influence. In science-fiction a lot of things work on two levels. I studied English at university and was very interested in this, the allegory and extended metaphor. Also, at the time, musicals like 'Hair' were very influential. Take the Age of Aquarius, which was interpreted by many as being about free love and peace. I didn't see it that way. I saw a huge potential for the human race to be destructive – and we were seeing that with the Vietnam war. So these sorts of concepts were rattling around for me.[22]

Songs can work on two levels, and 'Out on the Street' does so. While fitting seamlessly into the album's wider concept, and here re-recorded to ensure that it sits sonically with what surrounds it (resulting in a superior version), as a single it had stood on its own merits in that very different context and soared to the top of the chart.

(The claim that the album version is superior is not universally held. Brent Eccles, for one, believes that re-recording 'Out on the Street' 'was a dubious move because even though it had better sounds on it the track ended up with half the magic'.[23])

Angel

Oh I'm beside myself – More than anything I'm trying to adjust my face

To believe your grace as you move around me
And when I start to scream – I'm really calling to you
And I don't want to score – I'm really bleeding for you

Goodbye Angel – Yes there's blood in my eyes, don't talk
I've been good – You always said I was *(Yes sir)*
I've tried Angel – There's nothing to fear, don't talk
Strike it hard, strike it fast, to believe I'm last
Crone on 2B world

God, it's black in the complex
Strange shapes in the doorways
The scene was black – the scream was still
An ancient instinct here still burning
So when I start to scream – I'm really calling to you
And I don't want to score – I'm really bleeding for you

Oh goodbye Angel – Yes there's blood in my eyes, don't talk
I've been good – You always said I was *(Yes sir)*
And I've tried Angel – There's nothing to fear, don't talk
It's hard when you're alone to be anything more than a gok
   and a clone

Oh yeah, goodbye Angel – Yes there's blood in my eyes, don't
   talk
I've been good – You always said I was *(Yes sir)*
I've tried Angel – There's nothing to fear, don't talk
It's hard to die though you're told it's a door to a new life

Goodbye Angel – don't you lose your head, yeah
The book may soon be read, no?
Don't do anything bad
Goodbye Angel – It's your heart

Side two begins with blips, bleeps, squeals and rumbles – futuristic, atmospheric and scene-setting. *Salient* reviewer MacLennan was not a fan, suggesting it 'starts off with some stupid noises from producer Alan Galbraith's ARP synthesiser, which are quite superfluous'.[24] Blanx took a similarly negative view, complaining that the synthesizer mimicked Brian Eno.[25] Nonessential these sounds may have been, but they also fit the context, and one can't help wondering if such accusations would have been levelled at an Emerson, Lake and Palmer album.

To the thousands who'd purchased the single of 'Out on the Street', 'Angel' was familiar territory as it was the B side. Like its more famous stablemate, the album version is superior. With the synthesizer having set the scene, when the song proper kicks in, it does so suddenly and powerfully with its snare, bass and power chord approximation of a flamenco rhythm (ta da, ta daa!).

'Angel' is an example of straightforward heavy rock music of its day, where subtlety is subservient to power, punch and attitude. The lyrics retain Riddell's trademark flair but are nowhere near as flowery as 'Seabird' or 'Beautiful Boy'. Simpler music calls for things to be simpler all round. There is neither the time nor space for anything too flashy because the directness of the message – both musical and lyrical – would be compromised. It's a surprise, therefore, that MacLennan should choose this song to take Riddell to task: 'One criticism I have of Riddell is that he is too verbose lyrically.'[26]

This is not to say 'Angel' lacks the ability to deliver unexpected moments. The eleven-quaver scale hook that delineates the sectional changes is one. Another is the surprise upward key change that announces the song's outro, ensuring an ending well away from the sonic territory of all that preceded it.

With its obvious science-fiction references ('2B world', 'gok and a clone'), 'Angel' both strengthens and furthers Riddell's overarching fantasy theme with a clear tension evident between the human and technologically engineered poles. The song's plaintive and emotionally delivered final three words, 'It's your heart', strike at the core of the album's theme; does an engineered being such as a clone even possess such a thing?

Open Up

They amaze me – They know I care
But many times now they've questioned my belief in you
And they perturb me – Divulged my goal is bare
To refute the roles of any imposed false similitude *(and the helpful will say)*
You're a lot like him – Go on this way
We know it pays – It's the only way
Gold is never wrong – Haven't we said so all along?
Then they'll curse their lives and they'll kick the pricks
Subjected by their own demise

Chorus:
Open up! Open up!
The Philistine minds of a time we could transcend but our hands are tied in fear
Open up! Open up!
Tied and bound in fear over death's domain and they'll go around again and again

Open up! Open up!

Perhaps until the time – the right time comes, then they will
    see

If you walk pure roads – Revealing mystic codes one by one

Is it won by one – Do you learn in parts or know the parts as
    a whole?

It seems martyrs die for the causes – The only rights they can see

But heroes only die to appease and humour righteous gods

Oh, not forsaken – No fame had made them careless of their
    mark

It was a mistake to kill – But still they did at will

Then they criticized but still justified charades too involved to
    see, by most

Repeat chorus

Will the years go rolling on until we die and are we born again?

And if the years keep rolling on and we are born again

Do we just go around again or can we see it all? – Can we be
    it all?

My brother says he knows

Repeat chorus

The slow-paced 'Open Up' begins with Riddell's signature double-tracked lead guitar establishing a strong melodic hook, one that returns again after the first chorus and before the second verse. The pace allows for further mining of his image-rich lyrics, a point noted by Blanx but clearly not to his pleasure:

Roget's Thesaurus open on the table, a few ideas filtered through half-realised concept and an assumed street sensibility – the weaknesses that make a song like Bowie's 'Time' a little too close to pastiche to be true. Thank god for Ronson in that case and Riddell isn't Ronson (though at times he tries very hard). Bowie always had Ronson to check his tendency to excess.[27]

Again, I believe this is not a weakness of Riddell's but, rather, a significant strength. A line such as 'To refute the roles of any imposed false similitude' has a quality that cannot be easily dismissed.

Clark's rhythm guitar is to the fore in 'Open Up', its steady and simple chug locking the components together throughout; the chicka-chick of plectrum on strings almost hypnotic. 'Open Up' is simple and unembellished in an instrumental sense compared to much of the album's content; the bridge section presents the listener with the clearest expression yet of Riddell's pre-eminent theme. Set up once again by an uplifting harmonic shift, the bridge does exactly what it is supposed to do in the songwriter's craft, that is, change the protagonist's perspective. Here, Riddell launches the BIG existential question in language that is markedly, cleverly, suddenly direct: 'And if the years keep rolling on and we are born again. / Do we just go around again or can we see it all?' Furthering the impact of this most challenging of questions, Riddell's voice takes on a beseeching, almost pleading, quality that demonstrates amply the extraordinary emotive range of which he is capable.

Riddell may have been disappointed that time ran out before completing the recording of the backing vocals from his bandmates, but here on 'Open Up' there is no issue. The all-male backing vocals fade in to become a feature of the outro.

Scars of Love

Flights and fancy flashing turn the lights so low
Our loves a pulsed synchro-mashing
I know a place we can go – We'll be free from all hyping
So far out – let things flow

Mmm my sister – you just about missed
A show that was made for you – A play that the boys like too

We're half cut on moonbeams – Spaced out baby I'll show
It's so tight it soon seems we'll be sailing further than you know
Harmony you might find – Ecstasy you may find

Oh well my sister when the question comes 'Do you want in?'
Do you know what you'll say?

Chorus:
They're only scars of love
They're saviour scars of love
And scars like this ain't frightening when they come from
 above

Oh your prima-donna baby is looking so fine tonight
And the air is mauve and hazy – You'll develop psychic sights
And if you can't control the feeling then the plan is going right

Oh my sister – you just about missed
A show that was made for you – A play that the boys like too

Finally if you're intact – survived the utility dream
It's the fin de siecle then you won't have to scream
'Cos now that we're phased out – Now the deal's almost
 through

Well my sister when the question comes 'Do you want in?'
Do you know what you'll say?

Repeat chorus

Selected as the B side of the 'Fräulein Love' single, the second shortest song on the album at three minutes and twenty-eight seconds found instant favour with David MacLennan in *Salient*. The reviewer was emboldened to go further than most would have dared in the seemingly obligatory Bowie-comparison portion of his appraisal:

> Then we come to the finest slab of pure rock ever made in New Zealand – 'Scars of Love'. This song is simply marvellous. A strong, stomping rocker with an extremely catchy guitar line and a great chorus all of which is underlaid by a strong fuzz guitar/cowbell beat. This should have been the next single. Eats 'Queen Bitch' and 'Suffragette City' for breakfast![28]

A very different view of Eccles' cowbell was expressed by Blanx in *Hot Licks*, however. Regarding its presence as 'an irritant', he went further, 'One day the patent cowbell bomp will be outlawed from popular music and will anyone be sorry?'[29]

'Scars of Love' shares the I-II-IV chord sequence of 'Fräulein Love' in its verses, before employing rock's staple I, IV and V chords in the chorus. Highly diatonic throughout, it's the last of the album's four-on-the-floor rock tracks, heavy and unrelenting throughout but none the worse for that given its direct, this-is-what-you-get honesty. That said, complete predictability is once again avoided by the employment of a rhythmic variation in the verses. Standard rock dictates a snare hit on the two and four, but here Eccles, supported by the other musicians, brings in that second snare hit half a beat earlier (on the three *and*).

Science-fiction imagery is to the fore, while the employment of the French term *fin de siècle* (the end of the century) adds a touch of Riddell's intellectual refinement that it's hard to imagine any other Kiwi rock musician employing either then or since. Special mention should be made of the opening line. The (almost) consecutive Fs of the words 'Flights of Fancy Flashing' – each one set to a full crotchet on the first three beats of the bar and thus ensuring maximum power of delivery – illustrate nicely the alliteration that Riddell relishes. As mentioned, using words for their sound as much as for their meaning is a Riddell strength and a point of uniqueness often overlooked or lost in accusations of over-wordiness.

And Up To Now

> I've been searching for a long time – But Simon, god he knows
> Spending worried days and fretful hours – research the lives of
> programmed clones
> But no I've never read where it's been said that there is a
> possibility
> That D stream guys with green stain eyes could possibly
> perceive of love
> And when at first I felt the goads of an impulse not allowed for
> I buried them through fear that there was something to be
> proud of
> But in recent days I weighed the chance – Perhaps there was
> another who

Although it's banned, or at least not planned, felt much the
    same as me

Chorus:
And up to now I never never thought I'd find someone like
    you
And up to now I always always thought I'd like a love, it's true

My prototype is Robert – He looks a lot like me
But he's much much older, forty-two, and I'm twenty-three
And when I asked if he'd ever had a response intuitively
He said if he had he would have programmed it into MDU3

But I'm not at all like Robert apart from slight identicalities
There's nothing more to explain the score – The when and
    whys of you and me
And so we'll meet, and sweet I think we should marry secretly
And quietly work to build a love in which it's blissful just to be

Repeat chorus

If there's one track that risks overstepping the mark in its
wordiness, it is 'And Up To Now'. It was the final track recorded,
and, due to a combination of dwindling time and its complexity,
it ended up being recorded faster than intended. Eccles writes:

Three days were set aside to record the rhythm tracks which
we managed to do by the skin of our teeth. . . . We were down
to our last track which was 'Rock & Roll America' (this track is
titled 'And Up To Now' on the album). It took a little longer than
the rest to get right. . . . Finally we got the one that everyone
said yes to. It was so fast it wasn't funny, as Alastair was to find
out when it came to vocal time.[30]

The pace of the lyrics is intense, and Riddell's opportunities for drawing breath are limited. A line such as 'D stream guys with green stain eyes' – notable for its carefully chosen alliterative and rhyming qualities – becomes a tongue-twister. That he pulls it off is admirable, but without recourse to the lyric sheet, the listener at times may struggle to discern the message the verses convey.

There are several techniques a songwriter can employ to ensure a chorus stands out from a song's verses. One technique is rhythmic augmentation or diminution; that is, respectively, the use of longer or shorter notes. Thankfully, given the foregoing discussion, Riddell chose augmentation for the chorus melody of 'And Up To Now', therefore this section with its drawn-out words provides relief.

The thematic premise of the album is to the forefront, with 'programmed clones' prominent and the human versus technology conundrum with its possibility of android love occurring throughout. The line 'He said if he had he would have programmed it into MDU3' requires further explanation. Riddell does: 'MDU-3 (Master Droid Unit 3) is a control computer/mind for all droids of a particular ilk.'[31]

Musically, Raynor stands out on this track; his Hammond organ solo late in the piece is virtuosic and thrilling. But the entire band deserves kudos here. Another highpoint is the interplay between drum fills and dramatic sonic stabs involving all instruments in the wonderfully syncopated outro.

Love the Way He Smiles

He could make the suns sing and they would sigh to ages
    spent in afternoons

Beyond this place – Our time or inviolate space
And he could fool the days pure as silver
Befriending the mercurial satin moon – And he often sang out
    of doors (And oh)

Chorus:
God! I love the way he smiles
He could make out so serene
God! I love the way he smiles
Where are your changes now? His truth has conquered time
Those peaceful eyes would gaze out at a world desperate full
    of aching hearts
Adrenaline poisoned from the start – Gifts to show us, some
    will never know

He could see the sauve qui peut behind the smiles
Of a race whose words were stagnant, stale and old
Whose paragon pride had waned, gone cold
And as he sang his tones assuaged my tears
A quietening balm to quell my fears
To help me see of what it is I am to be (And oh)

Repeat chorus
He would laugh and sing and my head would ring
My head would ring full of life light psalms
Appease all cries and false alarms
Spanning causal gaps born of rational minds
Released from concerns of peurile signs
And now I chant my sanguine lines (And oh)

At eight minutes and eight seconds, 'Love the Way He Smiles'
is another 'Seabird'-like epic, albeit far less formally structured
given that the last four minutes are highly improvisational.

In the first half and following a beautiful jazz-like opening of piano, bass and drums, the song oscillates between 4/4 and 2/4 sections, keeping the same overall tempo but with the latter passages giving the impression of a significant increase in speed, accompanied by rhythmic diminution in the vocal melody. From four minutes onwards, Raynor lets loose, and his extensive piano jam illustrates his talent. There is an apt expression in classical music: this is a ten-fingers-and-forelock performance. Galbraith too delves into his box of tricks, augmenting the track with crowd noises placed high in the mix while putting effects on Riddell's closing vocals, which are slowed to a drawl as they float amidst and around the randomly recurring words of the Yandall Sisters, who sing the title line with so much reverb it becomes ethereal. Through it all Cuddihy – exceptional on bass – and Eccles maintain a sense of order beneath the darkly carnivalesque goings-on. It's great stuff; a ride into the dangerous unknown that defies comparisons.

The Yandall Sisters almost manage to forge equal billing for themselves on 'Love the Way He Smiles', most especially in the chorus and latter parts of the song when their harmonized backing vocals soar. One can only imagine Riddell's delight when this classy addition was made to the mix.

Truly one of the stand-out tracks and certainly the most experimental and risky with its edge-of-your-seat vibe, 'Love the Way He Smiles' garnered almost universal praise from reviewers. Even, remarkably, from Blanx in *Hot Licks*:

'Love The Way He Smiles' is an amazingly ambitious number in the light of the rest of the album. It stands or falls on its production. Let's just say it teeters dangerously. But it does have a mysterioso feel to it that makes it immediately more interesting than its predecessors, suggesting that Alastair's real forte is the art rock realm of Genesis and Peter Hamill rather than Stooges-style street theatre.[32]

Thurgood's *Hot Licks* review was even more effusive, although clearly he was not so keen on the highly improvised outro: "'Love The Way He Smiles", apart from the indulgent last quarter, is the most powerful song on the album. I'll even go so far as to call it brilliant . . . this one really stands out as masterful music.'[33]

MacLennan also chose the song as his prime pick:

The album closes with 'Love The Way He Smiles' which musically is the most interesting on the record. The last half of the track is best, featuring some lovely piano work from Raynor and some tight bass/piano interplay. There is an almost dream-like quality about this last section with its chorused hip 'hip hoorays' and the background vocals (courtesy of the Yandall Sisters).[34]

That the album should end in this manner – in confusing and delightful disarray – seems apt. From the very start the listener has experienced a smorgasbord of concepts and imagery, an overarching science-fiction vibe, snippets of wide-ranging philosophies, beliefs, religious doctrines and so on, all delivered in an artfully embroidered vocabulary bordering on intelligently alien. This has all transpired atop musical forms and structures that ranged from the highly complex and sophisticated realm of progressive rock through to straightforward rock/pop. Simply, an enormous amount of information is offered to the listener with no clear and convenient linear assemblage or pathway, requiring instead their significant input. It's intelligent music that opens a two-way street between performer and audience – engagement and depth of thought – is required.

As Riddell says, 'Life is complicated and the world is complicated, so I didn't want to be too prescriptive. I didn't want to remove the participation of the listener from the process. You engage them in a way that gives them room to be a part of the universe you're creating.'[35]

6 What came after

In early December 1974, soon after *Studio One/New Faces* but prior to recording their album, Space Waltz completed a highly successful six-date national tour, sponsored by EMI. Brent Eccles recalls:

> The venues were the Opera House, Palmerston North, the Opera House, Wellington, Nelson's Trafalgar Centre, the Christchurch Town Hall, Dunedin's Regent Theatre and the Civic Theatre in Invercargill. Alastair was very excited about the prospect of playing this tour as it had always been his dream to play these kinds of venues. Peter Cuddihy wanted to hold onto the security of his club gig so Mike Chunn came in on bass. Most of the shows on the tour were capacity audiences. I think we played to seven thousand people in the six days. By the time we hit Invercargill we were without exception totally fucked. It certainly wasn't total glamour all the way. But apart from being incredibly tired I had enjoyed every aspect of the experience.[1]

After the Wellington show, under the headline 'Space Waltzed Rock Fans into New Orbit', Bill Taylor wrote in the *Evening Post*:

> The excitement was put back into New Zealand rock music last night in the Opera House at the debut Wellington concert of the top New Zealand group, Space Waltz. It has been a long

time since a local group with such originality and freshness has appeared on the scene and the near capacity audience of 1387 clapped, cheered, stamped and whistled their appreciation. Lead singer and guitarist Alastair Riddell, the most exciting and original rock star in the country, led the group to great heights.[2]

An anonymous reviewer for the Christchurch *Press* was equally enthusiastic:

> 'Let there be music', he said. And there was music and it was good. For about an hour and a half the magic continued, sometimes harsh and raunchy, sometimes light and airy but always alive . . . visually, they were exciting, especially with the use of coordinated stage lighting. Most action came from Riddell who, for the first half of the performance, pouted and smiled with a mouth that matched his red tie. He pranced about in an olive, canary and pink candy-stripe suit. For the second half he sauntered and leapt about the stage in black, plum and gold velvet. He cast disdainful eyes at his delighted audience, then raised a hand to his forehead in mock shame.[3]

In addition to performances at the popular Buck-a-Head concerts and other one-off shows in 1975, the band undertook two further tours after recording their album. The first of these, limited to the North Island, was organized by Eccles – today an award-winning promoter and tour organizer – in conjunction with Radio New Zealand. Then in June the final Space Waltz tour was undertaken with the backing of the New Zealand Student Arts Council, comprising shows at the country's six universities.

Unlike the triumphant first tour, issues arose on these subsequent tours – some beyond the control of the band – that took a significant toll. Meanwhile relations between Riddell and EMI soured greatly. Although beyond the scope of this book, cracks were beginning to show.

In October 1975 the band moved to Melbourne after two personnel changes. Paul Baeyertz replaced Tony Raynor, who had decided earlier in the year to commit full time to Split Enz. Newly engaged Greg Clark, meanwhile, had made the decision to stay in New Zealand and was replaced by Dave Walker. Roger Jarrett in *Hot Licks* recorded the moment:

> In the early hours of Friday, October 31, Alastair Riddell and his band Space Waltz left Mangere for Melbourne, Australia and . . . 'fame'? For several months now since the completion of his North Island tour Alastair has been very quiet and had in fact announced his retirement from the 'New Zealand rock scene'. The tour hadn't gone that well, he was and is disappointed with the album *Space Waltz*. . . . The band have no guarantee of gigs but have had good feedback from the album from various sources. 'I have no pretentions that we're going to go over there to become an overnight success, but I do believe we can cut it.'[4]

Events quickly spiralled downwards in Australia with no work forthcoming and disagreements over management. After declining the opportunity to relocate to the UK with ambitious young promoter Michael Browning in the company of another up-and-coming band, AC/DC, a decision opposed by Riddell, by the year's end everyone except Riddell had returned home.

The Space Waltz story had ended unhappily. The full story will no doubt yet be told.

Individually, Riddell and the others would go on to many further notable achievements. Indeed, one of the oft-overlooked aspects of Space Waltz is how the band acted as a spawning ground, contributing musicians to a host of top Australasian bands. Eccles would go on to perform with Vox Pop, Street Talk, Citizen Band and the Angels. Cuddihy's future acts included Kindred Spirit, The Human Instinct and Street Talk. Raynor would record with Paul McCartney and tour with Crowded House, as well as being a member of Split Enz, Schnell Fenster, The Conrays, The Makers, Forenzics, Double Life, The Magnificent 7 and Another Life. Clark's acts included Vox Pop, Citizen Band, The Scanners, Khutze Band and the Wide Lapels.

Art rock

In the *Sydney Morning Herald* in 2021, Eddie Raynor mused on his musical tastes. He noted, 'I've always been drawn to complex, sophisticated music. I loved bands like Yes and Genesis. Prior to Split Enz, I was in a prog rock band called Space Waltz.'[5]

For all the glam appeal of 'Out on the Street' on *Studio One/ New Faces*, the album is a far more complex creation. Riddell confirmed:

We were very prog. When Paul Crowther, Eddie and myself got together in Orb in late '71 we were thinking progressive rock. But I realised that was going to have limited appeal. And you can do something really exciting with condensing ideas. It's even more thrilling in a way than going through these musical sagas, which was what Orb's set was like; just four songs and each one ten or twelve minutes long [*laughs*]. So, yes it's a progressive album – definitely. But I thought, 'If I want to get through to people I've got to make the songs shorter.'[6]

Make them shorter Riddell may have done, but with two songs running over eight minutes and an average track length of five minutes, it's a long way from the likes of Bowie and Bolan's glam-era work. Their *Ziggy Stardust* and *Electric Warrior* albums, respectively, for instance, average three and a half minutes per track.

Track length in itself, of course, is not a conclusive indicator, but compositional sophistication is. Aside from 'Out on the Street', 'Fräulein Love', 'Scars of Love' and 'Angel', the remaining five tracks are extremely intricate.

Labels such as glam and progressive carry connotations of aesthetic value. In the 1970s the two were seen as largely oppositional, with progressive equating to substance and complexity, and glam being light-weight and disposable.

In 1995 Gary Steel briefly discussed Space Waltz in a historical appraisal of New Zealand progressive rock, including them primarily because they used a Mellotron. He added, 'Space Waltz hardly rate a mention here, despite a slightly prog influence . . . [because] they were primarily influenced by the Glam movement and especially Bowie.'[7] Riddell, however, never saw such a division: 'Glam rock was in lots of ways a child of prog rock. People like Mick Ronson were looking in that direction. There are exceptions to that on the more inane end of it, of course, but it was posturing in a post-modern, futuristic way.'[8]

Now and then an act managed to successfully straddle the two – Roxy Music in particular. For their ilk, another term was employed: 'art rock'. Introduced to their debut album by a friend in 1972, Riddell's response was an emphatic 'Yes! This is it! This is great!'[9] And when contemplating the first two Roxy Music albums, he wondered, 'Is it glam? Is it prog? It's certainly somewhere in between, isn't it?'[10]

Music critic and author Barney Hoskyns identifies that middle ground: 'Roxy were Glam for adults – or at least for smart, savvy students. . . . Roxy brought brains to the Glam rock party, bridging the gap between progressive art rock and disposable teen pop.'[11]

'Art rock', too, is surely the best descriptor for *Space Waltz by Alastair Riddell*.

Neither Riddell nor his colleagues shun being deemed New Zealand's premier glam rock act. After all, it's a significant accolade. But they've never characterized themselves that way. In Riddell's case, he insists that he was simply 'an artist experimenting with ideas'.[12]

The depth and extent of the themes explored in the album, the style of language used, the quality of musicianship and the compositional complexity of the songs, all back up this notion of experimenting with a very deep well of ideas, some that had been under consideration for a long time. Riddell revealed, 'In the sixties when I first started playing in bands I had a four track tape recorder, because I was doing Art History and I was interested in Stockhausen and Musique Concrète and the experimental music that had come through from the fifties.'[13]

Where did this thirst for knowledge and desire for deep exploration come from?

> I am naturally an intellectual. In New Zealand, particularly, being an intellectual is still not a great thing, so you tend to hide your light under a bushel. My parents were intellectuals, and my mother used to say to me, 'Don't be ashamed to think about things; to think about ideas.' And she used to say, 'In this country you are likely to get your head beaten down more often than not, but it doesn't mean to say you shouldn't do it.'[14]

A final word on the Bowie thing

Space Waltz by Alastair Riddell was released when albums by New Zealand rock bands sold poorly with the nation still in the grip of the Cultural/Colonial Cringe. As music historian Chris Bourke has observed, this 'ingrained "cultural cringe" still meant their music was regarded as somehow second-rate to what they heard from England and America'.[15] Historian Naomi O'Connor notes the predominant view at the time was 'New Zealand's culture was an antipodean (and inferior) version of Britain's'.[16] As a result, the demand for local albums was low; Adam Holt, the current chairman of Universal Music New Zealand, explains that most albums consequently 'were only ever pressed once (usually an initial order of 500 units) and then deleted'.[17]

Because of the inevitable value judgement directed at local artists, the first reaction from critics and the public was to compare them to 'the real thing' overseas. Thus, from the first moment the camera focused on Alastair Riddell on *Studio One/New Faces*, accusations began that he was a David Bowie clone/copycat. And they never ceased. 'An antipodean David Bowie', 'a David Bowie clone', 'a David Bowie imitator' – these descriptors have been repeated in critiques of Riddell spanning almost fifty years. And, similarly, Space Waltz has been labelled simply as glam rock.

'I love David Bowie!' enthused Riddell in an interview in 2002.[18] Always happy to admit his admiration, Riddell nevertheless finds the fixation to pin him to Bowie–and–glam-rock rankling because his influences and the musical style(s) he subsequently developed stretched far beyond any single act or genre. Indeed, straight after his Bowie comment above, he went on to enthuse with equal passion about progressive rock band Yes. Riddell's favourite acts of the early seventies, prior to forming Space Waltz, reveal considerable breadth in his musical tastes. Yes, Kraftwerk, Tangerine Dream, Genesis, King Crimson, David Bowie, Jacques Brel, Roxy Music and Van der Graaf Generator are just some of the influences he was soaking up. To solely choose Bowie as the touchstone when appraising Riddell and his work is overly simplistic. Bowie's influence is strong, but one must go further. As music writer Grant Gillanders pointed out, 'One couldn't help but notice a Bowie influence but it was obvious that there was something deeper going on here, this wasn't a blatant Bowie copiest [*sic*], the song and group came across as too intelligent for that.'[19]

Riddell has commented further. He notes, 'David Bowie never wrote a song even vaguely like "Out on the Street". It has a swing chorus and a half-time verse. Jacques Brel and Peter Hamill [Van der Graaf Generator] were at least as big an influence on me, but in New Zealand all anyone could ever hear was Bowie. He was the only reference point we had.'[20]

With all of this said, because Riddell's impact on *Studio One/New Faces* was as startlingly visual as it was aural, his performative style, stagecraft and costuming was the focus of the nation's collective gaze as much as his music was. So, to challenge Riddell's comment a little, it was perhaps not so much New Zealanders *hearing* Bowie as seeing him. Or, at least, seeing reference points. Riddell even bore a passing physical resemblance to the English artist. His high cheekbones and aquiline features, glam-style costuming, make-up, long hair and exaggerated theatrical performance style ensured that comparison was not difficult to make. And so it was made without hesitation.

Further, Riddell's singing style could also be laid at Bowie's door to an extent. Simon Sweetman described Riddell's style as a 'gushy vocal which drips vowel sounds in a sardonic form of assonance'.[21] The highly affected, even pretentious delivery, complete with decidedly un-Kiwi-like exaggerated vowel sounds, bore a resemblance to what musicologist Alan Moore described as Bowie's 'fey vocals'.[22] But again that is overly simplistic because, while still a boy, Riddell enjoyed listening to his parents' Anthony Newley records long before David Bowie ever came on the scene. It is from Newley, the English actor, singer, songwriter and satirist, that Bowie is widely held to have developed his own vocal style.

Alan Galbraith sums up the situation well. He suggests, 'The influence versus copying thing is a pet peeve of mine. I believe all musical artists influence each other. It's the same with songs. Everything in pop music is derivative.'[23]

But, yes, there's no denying Alastair Riddell and Space Waltz could be aligned to David Bowie and glam rock with relative ease when judged solely on their *Studio One/New Faces* debut. However, the bigger picture was never as clear-cut, and the album exemplifies this.

First impressions stick firmly, and that initial Bowie-and-glam-rock pigeon-holing would prove extremely hard to break down as Riddell progressed in his career. Consider this subsequent review from 1977:

> The latest product of new local label, Mandrill, is a single for Alastair Riddell. Shedding the Space Waltz front, Riddell has virtually single-handedly produced a remarkable little piece – 'Wonder Ones'. The jerky piano intro and characteristic harmony guitar work are the most prominent thing about the early stages of the song, until a really great chorus sweeps in to carry all before it. Of course it sounds a little too close in lyrical content to 'Oh, You Pretty Things' to be completely comfortable.[24]

In the public consciousness, Alastair Riddell was firmly 'that David Bowie guy'.

Of all the reviewers who appraised the Space Waltz album at the time of its release, Brian Thurgood best seemed to avoid the Cultural Cringe trap. He wrote:

> Similar starting points can develop to similar results. By this I mean – if you are a classical composer and you set out to write a Messiah, chances are you'll develop the musical form you think best suits such a concept, your results bearing some resemblance to other's work in the same form. Similarly, if you set out to write a hit single, the results are likely to be similar to many others' results. Alastair,

being a skilled and thoughtful musician, being of a philosophical bent, and being rather perceptive of our society and its possible evolutions, problems, values etc, has created music that is similar to others who have started from such foundations. Thus, comparison with Bowie, Roxy Music and Split Enz will show many similarities – Space Waltz stands beside the music of such people. It is not the same, certainly not a copy, and doesn't necessarily owe much to the others in terms of influence even.[25]

And in conclusion

In 1978 in *Rip It Up*, Riddell said that he considered his then-forthcoming album to be his solo debut. He described *Space Waltz by Alastair Riddell* as 'a pretty rushed and confused affair. I put a lot into writing the songs but what came out was pretty disillusioning'.[26] Further, he enthusiastically observed of the new album: 'It's a beginning, a restarting and that's the way I feel about it.'[27]

Today, with prevailing attitudes towards locally produced art across all mediums enormously different from those almost five decades ago, it is evident that the album is far better appreciated. Simon Grigg remarks: 'When we formed the Suburban Reptiles, our calling came more from the likes of Space Waltz than ever it did from the Ramones and the Sex Pistols. It's hard to overstate how important that record was to the future.'[28] Further, Grigg believes:

It remains a landmark recording, successfully straddling the gap between the glam-pop of the hit and the next single, 'Fraulein Love', and the lyrically and sonically more adventurous tracks like 'Angel' and 'Love the Way he Smiles'. [It is] one of the great New Zealand albums.[29]

Others support this view. Graham Reid opines, 'It's courageously outré, musically ambitious . . . a cultural touchstone located between ambitiously poetic glam rock and prog-pop [and] is still enjoyably transporting.'[30] Record collectors Gordon and Janis Stevenson enthuse: "Its stand-out mix of glam, prog and dystopian themes of science fiction were like nothing seen in the Southern hemisphere at the time, and it has endured as a cult classic."[31] Nick Bollinger suggests:

> Space Waltz dragged New Zealand rock out of a desert of blue denim and blues licks, where the music had been languishing since the late sixties, and there would be no going back. And yet the advent of punk less than two years later meant it would remain unique in the country's discography; a solitary monument to Alastair Riddell's stubborn and extravagant vision.[32]

Of course, with the perspective that time brings, Riddell today is immensely proud of the album, as are Cuddihy, Raynor, Eccles and Clark. Riddell, however, can't help but continue to speculate on what might have been if things had worked out differently: 'I think if Space Waltz had gone to England we'd have been a bigger band than Split Enz.'[33]

Associate Professor Robert Burns, progressive rock specialist and newcomer to Space Waltz's unique Kiwi blend of progressive rock and glam, opined something similar. He suggests, 'If they'd been managed in a different way and had been in Britain around '74/'75, I think it could have been a very different story.'[34]

New Zealand Listener writer Dominic Blaazer agrees. He observes, 'Space Waltz was acutely contemporary with 1974's UK pop scene, and things would have been altogether different had they found themselves amongst peers like Roxy Music, T-Rex [*sic*] and yes, okay, David Bowie.'[35]

It's a moot point, of course, but take a moment to ponder a poignant comment from Eddie Raynor as he looked back on the journey into the unknown that he took with his friend Alastair Riddell. Raynor recollects, 'We were just a bunch of kids who had no experience in such things and nothing to relate it to. We were just having fun being in a band.'[36]

The passage of time has afforded Riddell and Space Waltz some (over)due recognition, as subsequent generations have come to realize and appreciate what earlier musical trailblazers, such as they, achieved. As Naomi O'Connor attests, 'Individuals who braved the derision and suspicion with which New Zealand's generally very physically-orientated society greeted any possibly esoteric or pretentious artistic endeavour, laid the foundations for later generations to build a local culture.'[37]

Alastair Riddell is not New Zealand's David Bowie. He is New Zealand's Alastair Riddell. And *Space Waltz by Alastair Riddell* is a landmark recording.

Watch out, young love . . .

Postscript

Remarkably, Space Waltz reformed in 2021 with all original members present. *Space Waltz by Alastair Riddell* is scheduled for re-release by Universal Music New Zealand Ltd in June 2022, albeit with a slightly altered track order to even out the timing of the two sides and thus accommodate today's rather different requirements for vinyl pressings. In addition, an album of entirely new material has been written and recorded and is due for release in late 2022/early 2023.

Notes

Chapter 2

1 Dominic Blaazer, '"Takin" It Back to the Street', *New Zealand Musician*, June/July 1998, 30.

2 Roger Jarrett, 'Editorial', *Hot Licks*, December 1974/January 1975, 3.

3 Bruce Sheridan and Philip Hayward, 'Let's Go to Frenzy: A Brief History of New Zealand Music TV and Music Video', in *North Meets South: Popular Music in Aotearoa/New Zealand*, ed. Philip Hayward, Tony Mitchell and Roy Shuker (Wellington: Perfect Beat Publications, 1994), 112.

4 Chris Bourke, *Crowded House: Something So Strong* (Sydney: Macmillan Publishing, 1997), 14.

5 Mike Chunn, *Stranger than Fiction: The Life and Times of Split Enz* (Wellington: GP Publications, 1992), 57.

6 Ibid.

7 Sheridan and Hayward, 'Let's Go to Frenzy', 112.

8 Alastair Riddell, email to the author, 27 June 2002.

9 Alastair Riddell, *Kiwi Gold Hit Disc 2* (Wellington: Hit or Miss Productions, New Zealand on Air, 1998). Nb) Tawa is a suburb of Wellington.

10 Wade Ronald Churton, *Have You Checked the Children* (Christchurch: Put Your Foot Down Publishing, 2001), 15.

11 Don McGlashan, Qtd in *Anthems: New Zealand's Iconic Hits* (Auckland: Notable Pictures, 2019).

12 Grant Smithies, *Soundtrack: 118 Great New Zealand Albums* (Nelson: Craig Potton Publishing, 2007), 159.

13 Nick Bollinger, *Goneville: A Memoir* (Wellington: Awa Press, 2016), 83.

14 Gary Steel, email to the author, 21 February 2022.

15 Simon Grigg, email to the author, 18 March 2022.

16 Sheridan and Hayward, 'Let's Go to Frenzy', 112.

17 'Two Series Combined', *New Zealand Listener*, 24 August 1974, 13.

18 Riddell, email, 27 June 2002.

19 Alastair Riddell, 'Out on the Street', in *Glory Days: From Gumboots to Platforms*, ed. Ian Chapman (Auckland: Harper Collins, 2009), 64.

20 Riddell, email, 27 June 2002.

21 Alan Galbraith, email to the author, 22 August 2021.

22 Alastair Riddell, Qtd in Nick Bollinger, *Audioculture*, https://www.audioculture.co.nz/profile/alastair-riddell (accessed 31 March 2022).

23 Graeme Downes, email to the author, 14 March 2022.

24 Riddell, 'Out on the Street', 65.

Chapter 3

1 Roger Watkins, *Hostage to the Beat: The Auckland Scene 1955–1970* (Auckland: Tandem Press, 1995), 124.

2 Alastair Riddell, 'Musical Chairs', *Radio New Zealand*, 6 July 2002.

3 Brent Eccles, email to the author, 13 September 2021.

4 Ibid.

5 Alastair Riddell, 'Reeling in the Years', *Radio New Zealand*, 17 November 2009.

6 Ibid.

7 Eccles, email, 13 September 2021.

8 Ibid.

9 Riddell, 'Reeling in the Years'.

10 Eccles, email, 13 September 2021.

11 Ibid.

Chapter 4

1 Alan Galbraith, Qtd in Simon Grigg, 'Alan Galbraith Part 1: From Nelson to HMV', *Audioculture*, https://www.audioculture.co.nz/articles/alan-galbraith-part-1-from-nelson-to-hmv (accessed 11 March 2022).

2 Alan Galbraith, 'Musical Chairs: Alan Galbraith Part Two', *Radio New Zealand*, https://www.rnz.co.nz/national/programmes/musicalchairs/audio/201860475/musical-chairs-alan-galbraith-part-two (accessed 11 March 2022).

3 Galbraith, Qtd in Grigg, 'Alan Galbraith Part 1'.

4 Alan Galbraith, 'Alan Galbraith: Making Records at HMV and EMI', *Audioculture*, https://www.audioculture.co.nz/articles/alan-galbraith-making-records-at-hmv-and-emi (accessed 11 March 2022).

5 Michael Grafton-Green, 'Musical Chairs', *Radio New Zealand*, 22 June 2013.

6 Alan Galbraith, email to the author, 10 March 2022.

7 Alastair Riddell, Zoom interview with the author, 22 March 2022.

8 Ibid.

9 Tony Aspland, email to the author, 19 September 2021.

10 Ibid.

11 Riddell, Zoom interview, 22 March 2022.

12 Ibid.

13 Ibid.

14 Alastair Riddell, email to the author, 9 September 2021.

15 Ibid.

16 Peter Cuddihy, phone interview with the author, 4 March 2022.

17 Peter Cuddihy, email to the author, 4 September 2021.

18 Eccles, email, 13 September 2021.

19 Greg Clark, email to the author, 25 August 2021.

20 Cuddihy, email, 4 September 2021.

21 Riddell, Zoom interview, 22 March 2022.

22 Eddie Raynor, email to the author, 30 August 2021.

23 Alan Galbraith, email to the author, 22 August 2021.

24 Ibid.

25 Alan Galbraith, email to the author, 28 August 2021.

26 Alan Galbraith, email to the author, 16 February 2022.

27 Derek King, 'Alastair Riddell', *Hot Licks*, October 1974, 11.

28 Qtd in ibid.

29 Ray Columbus, 'Sound Round', *New Zealand Listener*, 30 November 1974, 24.

30 Eddie Raynor, email to the author, 21 September 2021.

31 Brent Eccles, email to the author, 23 November 2021.

32 Greg Clark, email to the author, 24 November 2021.

33 Cuddihy, phone interview, 4 March 2022.

34 Riddell, Zoom interview, 22 March 2022.

35 Ibid.

36 David MacLennan, 'New Zealand Artists are of High Standard', in *NZ Rock 'n Soul Review*, ed. Mike Alexander (Wellington: INL Print, 1976), 51.

37 'Double Track', *Sunday Times*, 1975, 36.

38 Brian Thurgood, 'A Riddle: A True Star?', *Hot Licks*, April 1975, 22.

39 Blanx, 'A Riddle: A True Star?', *Hot Licks*, April 1975, 22.

40 Rob White, 'Space Waltz LP Debut Rushed', *The Star*, 19 April 1975, 27.

41 MacLennan, 'New Zealand Artists are of High Standard', 51.

42 David MacLennan, 'Salient Album Review: Spacewaltz Featuring Alastair Riddell (EMI)', *Salient* 38, no. 4 (1975): 14.

43 Blanx, 'A Riddle', 22.

44 Alan Galbraith, 'Letters', *Hot Licks* 16 (1975): 9.

45 Don McGlashan, 'Bookmarking the Century', *Landfall* 199 (2000): 45.

46 Roger Page, Joan Cunliffe and John Ferris, 'Letters', *Hot Licks* 20 (1975): 5.

47 Roger Jarrett, 'Alastair Riddell Goes for Broke in Australia', *Hot Licks* 20 (1975): 7.

48 Blanx, 'A Riddle', 22.

49 Thurgood, 'A Riddle', 22.

50 MacLennan, 'Salient Album Review', 14.

51 Galbraith, 'Letters', 9.

52 Adam Holt, email to the author, 24 March 2022.

Chapter 5

1 Riddell, 'Out on the Street', 63–4.

2 Riddell, 'Musical Chairs'.

3 John F. Kennedy, 'Excerpt from the "Special Message to the Congress on Urgent National Needs"', *NASA*, https://www .nasa.gov/vision/space/features/jfk_speech_text.html (accessed 18 March 2022).

4 Robert Jones, 'They Came in Peace for All Mankind: Popular Culture as a Reflection of Public Attitudes to Space', *Space Policy* 20, no. 1 (2004): 47.

5 Riddell, 'Out on the Street', 64.

6 Riddell, *Kiwi Gold Hit Disc 2*.

7 Riddell, Zoom interview, 22 March 2020.

8 J. M. Cummings, 'Singles', *Hot Licks*, April 1975, 27.

9 Riddell, *Kiwi Gold Hit Disc 2*.

10 Riddell, Zoom interview, 22 March 2022.

11 Riddell, email, 27 June 2002.

12 Robert Burns, interview with the author, 31 March 2020.

13 Alastair Riddell, email to the author, 22 March 2022.

14 Ibid.

15 Francis Stark, 'Still Seasick after All these Years', *Rip It Up*, December 1977, 11.

16 Blanx, 'A Riddle', 22.

17 Cuddihy, phone interview, 4 March 2022.

18 Burns, interview.

19 Riddell, 'Out on the Street', 63.

20 Simon Sweetman, 'On Song with Simon Sweetman: Out on the Street', *Radio New Zealand*, 17 January 2013.

21 Qtd in Simon Sweetman, *On Song: Stories behind New Zealand's Pop Classics* (Auckland: Penguin, 2012), 171.

22 Ibid.

23 Eccles, email, 13 September 2021.

24 MacLennan, 'Salient Album Review', 14.

25 Blanx, 'A Riddle', 22.

26 MacLennan, 'Salient Album Review', 14.

27 Blanx, 'A Riddle', 22.

28 MacLennan, 'Salient Album Review', 14.

29 Blanx, 'A Riddle', 22.

30 Eccles, email, 13 September 2021.

31 Riddell, email, 27 June 2002.

32 Blanx, 'A Riddle', 22.

33 Thurgood, 'A Riddle', 22.

34 MacLennan, 'Salient Album Review', 14.

35 Riddell, Zoom interview, 22 March 2020.

Chapter 6

1 Eccles, email, 13 September 2021.

2 Bill Taylor, 'Space Waltzed Rock Fans into New Orbit', *Evening Post*, 4 December 1974, 27.

3 'Space Waltz Cast Spell over Town Hall', *Christchurch Press*, 7 December 1974, 31.

4 Jarrett, 'Alastair Riddell Goes for Broke in Australia', 7.

5 Qtd in Susan Skelly, 'History Never Repeats? New Project Sifts Split Enz's Gold Dust', *Sydney Morning Herald*, 12 November 2021, https://www.smh.com.au/culture/music/history-never-repeats-new-project-sifts-split-enz-s-gold-dust-20211106-p596l7.html (accessed 17 March 2022).

6 Riddell, Zoom interview, 22 March 2022.

7 Gary Steel, 'Godzone's Prog-Zone', *Real Groove*, July 1995, 16.

8 Riddell, Zoom interview, 22 March 2022.

9 Ibid.

10 Ibid.

11 Barney Hoskyns, *Glam: Bowie, Bolan and the Glitter Rock Revolution* (London: Faber and Faber, 1998), 56.

12 Alastair Riddell, email to the author, 29 August 2002.

13 Riddell, 'Musical Chairs'.

14 Riddell, Zoom interview, 22 March 2022.

15 Bourke, *Crowded House*, 14.

16 Naomi O'Connor, *New Zealand Art & Culture* (Nelson: Craig Potton Publishing, 1995), 6.

17 Adam Holt, email to the author, 28 March 2022.

18 Riddell, 'Musical Chairs'.

19 Grant Gillanders, liner notes, CD release, *Space Waltz by Alastair Riddell* (RPM Records, UK, 2005).

20 Qtd in Bollinger, *Goneville*, 90.

21   Sweetman, *On Song*, 174.

22   Alan F. Moore, 'Bowie, David', in *New Grove Dictionary of Music and Musicians Vol. 4*, ed. Stanley Sadie (London: Macmillan, 2001), 150.

23   Alan Galbraith, email to the author, 3 March 2022.

24   Francis Stark, 'Riddell Rides Again', *Rip It Up*, September 1977, 6.

25   Thurgood, 'A Riddle', 22.

26   Qtd in Alistair Dougal, 'Solo Riddell Out', *Rip It Up*, December 1978, 16.

27   Ibid.

28   Simon Grigg, email to the author, 19 March 2022.

29   Simon Grigg, 'Alan Galbraith Part 2: EMI and Beyond', *Audioculture*, https://www.audioculture.co.nz/articles/alan -galbraith-part-2-emi-and-beyond (accessed 8 April 2022).

30   Graham Reid, 'Stardust Memories: Recalling When Space Waltz Danced to Their Own Tune', *New Zealand Listener*, 7–13 August 2021, 63.

31   Gordon and Janis Stevenson, 'Spacewaltz by Alastair Riddell', *Just for the Record*, https://www.justfortherecord .co.nz/albums/space-waltz-space-waltz-by-alastair-riddell/ (accessed 31 March 2022).

32   Nick Bollinger, email to the author, 11 April 2022.

33   Riddell, Zoom interview, 22 March 2022.

34   Burns, interview, 31 March 2022.

35   Blaazer, 'Takin' It Back to the Street', 31.

36   Eddie Raynor, email to the author, 8 September 2021.

37   O'Connor, *New Zealand Art & Culture*, 6.

Bibliography

Anthems: New Zealand's Iconic Hits. Auckland: Notable Pictures, 2019.

Blaazer, Dominic. '"Takin" It Back to the Street'. *New Zealand Musician*, June/July 1998, 30.

Blanx. 'A Riddle: A True Star?' *Hot Licks*, April 1975, 22.

Bollinger, Nick. 'Alastair Riddell'. *Audioculture*, https://www.audio culture.co.nz/profile/alastair-riddell (accessed 31 March 2022).

Bollinger, Nick. *Goneville: A Memoir*. Wellington: Awa Press, 2016.

Bourke, Chris. *Crowded House: Something So Strong*. Sydney: Macmillan Publishing, 1997.

Chunn, Mike. *Stranger than Fiction: The Life and Times of Split Enz*. Wellington: GP Publications, 1992.

Churton, Wade Ronald. *Have You Checked the Children*. Christchurch: Put Your Foot Down Publishing, 2001.

Columbus, Ray. 'Sound Round'. *New Zealand Listener*, 30 November 1974, 24.

Cummings, J. M. 'Singles'. *Hot Licks*, April 1975, 27.

'Double Track'. *Sunday Times*, 20 April 1975, 35.

Dougal, Alistair. 'Solo Riddell Out'. *Rip It Up*, December 1978, 16.

Galbraith, Alan. 'Alan Galbraith: Making Records at HMV and EMI'. *Audioculture*, https://www.audioculture.co.nz/articles/ alan-galbraith-making-records-at-hmv-and-emi (accessed 11 March 2022).

Galbraith, Alan. 'Letters'. *Hot Licks* 16 (1975): 9.

Galbraith, Alan. 'Musical Chairs: Alan Galbraith Part Two'. *Radio New Zealand*, https://www.rnz.co.nz/national/programmes/ musicalchairs/audio/201860475/musical-chairs-alan-galbraith -part-two (accessed 11 March 2022).

Gillanders, Grant. *Liner Notes for Release on Compact Disc of Space Waltz by Alastair Riddell*. United Kingdom: RPM Records, 2005.

Grafton-Green, Michael. 'Musical Chairs'. *Radio New Zealand*, 22 June 2013.

Grigg, Simon. 'Alan Galbraith Part 1: From Nelson to HMV'. *Audioculture*, https://www.audioculture.co.nz/articles/alan -galbraith-part-1-from-nelson-to-hmv (accessed 11 March 2022).

Grigg, Simon. 'Alan Galbraith Part 2: EMI and Beyond'. *Audioculture*, https://www.audioculture.co.nz/articles/alan -galbraith-part-2-emi-and-beyond (accessed 8 April 2022).

Hoskyns, Barney. *Glam: Bowie, Bolan and the Glitter Rock Revolution*. London: Faber and Faber, 1998.

Jarrett, Roger. 'Alastair Riddell Goes for Broke in Australia'. *Hot Licks* 20 (1975): 7.

Jarrett, Roger. 'Editorial'. *Hot Licks*, December 1974/January 1975, 3.

Jones, Robert. 'They Came in Peace for All Mankind: Popular Culture as a Reflection of Public Attitudes to Space'. *Space Policy* 20, no. 1 (2004): 45–8.

Kennedy, John F. 'Excerpt from the "Special Message to the Congress on Urgent National Needs"'. *NASA*, https://www.nasa .gov/vision/space/features/jfk_speech_text.html (accessed 18 March 2022).

King, Derek. 'Alastair Riddell'. *Hot Licks*, October 1974, 11.

Kiwi Gold Hit Disc 2. Wellington: Hit or Miss Productions, New Zealand on Air, 1998.

MacLennan, David. 'New Zealand Artists Are of High Standard'. *NZ Rock 'n Soul Review*, 1976, 51–2.

MacLennan, David. 'Salient Album Review: Spacewaltz Featuring Alastair Riddell (EMI)'. *Salient* 38, no. 4 (1975): 37–8.

McGlashan, Don. 'Bookmarking the Century'. *Landfall* 199 (2000): 44–6.

Moore, Alan F. 'Bowie, David'. In *New Grove Dictionary of Music and Musicians Vol. 4*, edited by Stanley Sadie, 150. London: Macmillan, 2001.

O'Connor, Naomi. *New Zealand Art & Culture*. Nelson: Craig Potton Publishing, 1995.

Page, Roger, Joan Cunliffe and John Ferris. 'Letters'. *Hot Licks* 20 (1975): 5.

Reid, Graham. 'Stardust Memories: Recalling When Space Waltz Danced to Their Own Tune'. *New Zealand Listener*, 7–13 August 2021, 32.

Riddell, Alastair. 'Musical Chairs'. *Radio New Zealand*, 6 July 2002.

Riddell, Alastair. 'Out on the Street'. In *Glory Days: From Gumboots to Platforms*, edited by Ian Chapman, 63–5. Auckland: Harper Collins, 2009.

Riddell, Alastair. 'Reeling in the Years'. *Radio New Zealand*, 17 November 2009.

Sheridan, Bruce, and Philip Hayward. 'Let's Go to Frenzy: A Brief History of New Zealand Music TV and Music Video'. In *North Meets South: Popular Music in Aotearoa/New Zealand*, edited by Philip Hayward, Tony Mitchell and Roy Shuker, 111–21. Wellington: Perfect Beat Publications, 1994.

Skelly, Susan. 'History Never Repeats? New Project Sifts Split Enz's Gold Dust'. *Sydney Morning Herald*, 12 November 2021, https:// www.smh.com.au/culture/music/history-never-repeats-new -project-sifts-split-enz-s-gold-dust-20211106-p596l7.html (accessed 17 March 2022).

Smithies, Grant. *Soundtrack: 118 Great New Zealand Albums*. Nelson: Craig Potton Publishing, 2007.

'Space Waltz Cast Spell over Town Hall'. *The Press*, 7 December 1974, 31.

Stark, Francis. 'Riddell Rides Again'. *Rip It Up*, September 1977, 6.

Stark, Francis. 'Still Seasick after all these Years'. *Rip It Up*, December 1977, 11.

Steel, Gary. 'Godzone's Prog-Zone'. *Real Groove*, July 1995, 16–17.

Stevenson, Gordon, and Janis Stevenson. 'Spacewaltz by Alastair Riddell'. *Just for the Record*, https://www.justfortherecord .co.nz/albums/space-waltz-space-waltz-by-alastair-riddell/ (accessed 31 March 2022).

Sweetman, Simon. *On Song: Stories Behind New Zealand's Pop Classics*. Auckland: Penguin, 2012.

Sweetman, Simon. 'On Song with Simon Sweetman: Out on the Street'. *Radio New Zealand*, 17 January 2013.

Taylor, Bill. 'Space Waltzed Rock Fans into New Orbit'. *Evening Post*, 4 December 1974, 14.

Thurgood, Brian. 'A Riddle: A True Star?' *Hot Licks*, April 1975, 22.

'Two Series Combined'. *New Zealand Listener*, 24 August 1974, 13.

Watkins, Roger. *Hostage to the Beat: The Auckland Scene 1955– 1970*. Auckland: Tandem Press, 1995.

White, Rob. 'Space Waltz LP Debut Rushed'. *The Star*, 19 April 1975, 27.

Index

'And Up To Now'   33, 89–91

'Angel' (album track)   33, 81–4,
        101, 107–8

'Angel' (single)   83

art rock   6, 94, 100–3

Aspland, Tony   34, 40–1

Baeyertz, Paul   99

Baigent, Michael   34, 39–40

'Beautiful Boy' (album
        track)   33, 53, 70–3,
        83

'Beautiful Boy' (TV
        performance)   20–1,
        71–3

Blaazer, Dominic   109

Blanx   52, 54–7, 75–6, 83,
        85–6, 88, 93–4

Bolan, Marc   14, 73, 101

Bollinger, Nick   15, 108

Bourke, Chris   10, 103

Bourne, Chris   22, 23, 32

Bowie, David   4–5, 14, 16, 18,
        31, 53–5, 61, 67, 68,
        71, 80, 86, 88, 101,
        103–7, 109

Brel, Jacques   55, 58, 104–5

Burns, Robert   73, 77, 108

Chunn, Mike   10–11, 20, 48, 97

Churton, Wade Ronald   14

Clark, Greg   1, 6, 29, 31, 34,
        43, 44, 47–50, 86, 99,
        100, 108

Columbus, Ray   48–9

cover (album)   34, 39–42, 49

Crowther, Paul   27–8, 100–1

Cuddihy, Peter   1, 6, 25–7,
        29–31, 34, 42–5,
        47–50, 76, 77, 93, 97,
        100, 108

Cultural Cringe (aka Colonial
        Cringe)   51, 58,
        103–4, 106

Cummings, J. M.   68

Dawkins, Peter   35–6

Double Track   51–2

Downes, Graeme   23

Eccles, Brent   1, 6, 28–32, 34,
        43, 44, 47–50, 66, 76,
        81, 88–90, 93, 97, 98,
        100, 108

EMI   3, 22, 23, 34–8, 42–5, 47,
          48, 50, 58–60, 97, 99

Ferry, Bryan   54, 69
'Fräulein Love'   33, 53, 64–9, 72,
          73, 76, 88, 101, 107

Galbraith, Alan   6, 22, 34–9,
          43–7, 55–8, 77, 83,
          93, 105
Gillanders, Grant   104
glam rock   1, 4–7, 32, 46, 69,
          73, 79–80, 101–2,
          104–8
Grafton-Green, Michael   34,
          37–8
Grigg, Simon   16, 107–8

Hamill, Peter   61, 94, 104–5
Hayward, Philip   9–11, 17
Holt, Adam   59–60, 103
Hoskyns, Barney   102
Hughes, Steve   31

Jarrett, Roger   7–8, 57, 99

Karavias, Nick   17–21
Kielly, Steve   31
King, Derek   47–8

Little, Craig   11–12, 16–18,
          20, 47

'Love the Way He Smiles'   33,
          91–4, 107–8

McGlashan, Don   14, 56, 79
MacLennan, David   51, 53–4,
          57–8, 83, 88, 94
Morrison, Howard   17–21

New Faces   9–12
Newley, Anthony   105

O'Connor, Naomi   103, 109
O'Donnell, Paddy   17–19, 21
'Open Up'   33, 53, 84–6
Orb   27–8, 53, 75, 100–1
Original Sun   26
Original Sun Blues Band   25–6
'Out on the Street' (album
          track)   7, 33, 63, 72,
          77–81, 101, 104–5
'Out on the Street' (single)   3,
          7, 8, 22–4, 48, 68, 69,
          81, 107
'Out on the Street' (TV
          performance)   3, 4,
          7, 8, 11–12, 14–17, 19,
          21–4, 31, 32, 100

production   43–6, 57–9
progressive rock   1, 6, 27–8,
          51, 73, 75, 77, 94–5,
          100–2, 104, 108

Ragnarok   51, 59
Raynor, Tony (Eddie)   1, 6,
          27–31, 34, 43–5,
          47–50, 53, 69, 76, 91,
          93, 94, 99, 100, 108,
          109
reception   46, 50–9
recording   23, 38–9, 43–5
Reid, Graham   75, 108
Riddell, Ron   25–6
Ronson, Mick   86, 101
Roxy Music   53, 54, 56, 102,
          104, 107, 109

sales   8, 59–60
'Scars of Love'   33, 61, 87–9,
          101
'Seabird'   28, 33, 53, 73–7, 83
Sheridan, Bruce   9–11, 17
Smithies, Grant   14–15
Split Ends (Split Enz)   10–11,
          15, 28, 31, 47, 48, 55,
          59, 107, 108
Steel, Gary   15–16, 101

Stevenson, Gordon   108
Stevenson, Janis   108
Stewart and the
          Belmonts   29–32, 47
Studio One   9, 11, 17, 35
Studio One/New Faces   1, 4, 8–11,
          17, 21–2, 31–2, 47–8,
          50, 58, 64, 69, 106
Sweetman, Simon   79, 105

Taylor, Bill   97–8
Thurgood, Brian   52, 57, 94,
          106–7
tours   3, 48, 97–9

Walker, Dave   99
Warren, Phil   10–11, 17–21, 23
Watkins, Roger   26
White, Rob   52–3
Wilkinson, Paul (Wally)   27–8
'Wonder Ones'   106

Yandall Sisters   34, 38–9, 72,
          93, 94